AN INTRODUCTION TO THE STUDY OF HUMAN RIGHTS

An Introduction to the Study of Human Rights

BASED ON A SERIES OF LECTURES
DELIVERED AT KING'S COLLEGE, LONDON
IN THE AUTUMN OF 1970

Introduction by SIR FRANCIS VALLAT, K.C.M.G., Q.C.
Master of the Bench, Gray's Inn

EUROPA PUBLICATIONS : LONDON

EUROPA PUBLICATIONS LIMITED
18 Bedford Square, London, WC1B 3JN

© Sir Francis Vallat

ISBN (Cloth): 0 900 36255 3
(Paper): 0 900 36253 7
Library of Congress Catalog Card No. 72-89503

Printed and bound in England by
STAPLES PRINTERS LIMITED
at The Stanhope Press, Rochester, Kent

Contents

INTRODUCTION   vi
Professor Sir Francis Vallat of King's College, Professor
of International Law in the University of London

1. CHRISTIANITY AND HUMAN RIGHTS   1
The Reverend Canon Sydney Hall Evans, Dean of
King's College

2. THE RIGHTS OF MAN SINCE THE
REFORMATION: AN HISTORICAL SURVEY   16
Professor J. H. Burns, Professor of the History
of Political Thought, University of London

3. MAN AND THE MODERN STATE   *French text* 31
Professor René Cassin, formerly President of   *English text* 41
the European Court of Human Rights, founder of
the International Institute of Human Rights

4. RACE, POVERTY AND POPULATION (AN
INTERNATIONALIST'S VIEW)   52
The Right Honourable Lord Caradon, formerly
Minister of State and Permanent Representative of
the United Kingdom to the United Nations, New York

5. FREEDOM OF ASSOCIATION AND THE
RIGHT TO WORK   64
The Right Honourable Lord Denning, Master of the Rolls

6. THE RIGHT TO LIVE AND BE FREE   72
Professor J. E. S. Fawcett, Director of Studies,
Royal Institute of International Affairs, and
Vice-President of the European Commission of
Human Rights

7. THE LEGAL PROTECTION OF HUMAN
RIGHTS—NATIONAL AND INTERNATIONAL   83
Professor Sir Humphrey Waldock, member of the
International Law Commission and President of
the European Court of Human Rights

8. WAR AND HUMAN RIGHTS   99
Miss J. A. C. Gutteridge, formerly Legal Counsellor
in the Foreign Office

APPENDIX I   116
Extract from the Bill of Rights, 1688

APPENDIX II   118
Universal Declaration of Human Rights approved by
the General Assembly of the United Nations, 1948

BIBLIOGRAPHY   125

Introduction

PROFESSOR FRANCIS VALLAT

This Introduction deals with four matters. First, there is an explanation of the origin of the text. Secondly, there is a note on the principle of non-discrimination. Thirdly, there is also a note on the principle of self-determination. These notes are added because those two basic principles are not dealt with as such in the text of the book but in an approach to the study of human rights they deserve primary attention. Finally, there is a brief explanatory note about the Bibliography.

Text

The purpose of this book is to provide a short and easily read introduction to the study of human rights. It is based on a series of lectures delivered at King's College, London, in the autumn of 1970. The series of lectures was largely inspired by the purposes of the International Institution of Human Rights (René Cassin Foundation) established at Strasbourg in 1969. King's College, London, was one of the first members of the Institute – having joined in 1970.

It may be recalled here that the Institute is to serve as a centre for new initiatives and for stimulation, co-ordination, research and publication in the field of human rights. In particular, the Institute includes first among its aims the endeavour to develop the teaching of Human Rights in universities and law faculties by "the creation of specialist courses". Accordingly, it was considered appropriate in 1970 that King's College should have a series of lectures on human rights by highly qualified specialists and the series of lectures was arranged for the "Fridays at 10 Series" by Canon Evans, Dean of King's College, and by the author of this Introduction.

These lectures are not a miscellaneous collection. The series was designed to stimulate thought on various aspects of the subject but with a broad unity of theme. It was also intended that there should be some emphasis on European and particularly British aspects. Historically, Britain has made a great contribution to the cause of individual rights and liberties. Probably no people in the world has enjoyed such a large measure of personal liberty for such a long time as the English. Since the various editions of Magna Carta in the thirteenth century, English history has been studded with landmarks on the road of the development of the rights of the subject. Traditionally these rights have been set in the context of political freedom and the sovereignty of Parliament. As one example, an extract giving the main relevant provisions of the Bill of Rights 1688 is attached as Appendix I to this book.

It is a deplorable fact that the twentieth century has seen some of the most horrible crimes against humanity. But there has also been an enormous growth in respect for human rights and dignity. The recognition and protection of human rights has also been raised from the national to the international level. Of fundamental importance in this connection is the Universal Declaration of Human Rights approved by the General Assembly of the United Nations on 10 December 1948. That Declaration, which was proclaimed "as a standard of achievement for all peoples and for all nations", is attached as Appendix II to this book.

International agreements, constitutions, and other documents concerned with the definition and protection of human rights are now too numerous to mention here. However, there are three among them which are worthy of special attention and students of the subject are advised to focus their attention on them. These are:

(i) The European Convention for the Protection of Human Rights and Fundamental Freedoms of 4 November 1950, together with its Protocols.
(ii) The International Covenant on Economic, Social and Cultural Rights.
(iii) The International Covenant on Civil and Political Rights.

The second and third of these instruments were adopted by the General Assembly of the United Nations on 16 December 1966.

The documents mentioned above will be found in *Basic Documents on Human Rights* (1971), edited by Dr Ian Brownlie of Wadham College, Oxford. This collection of documents, which together with some useful notes and comments runs to some 525 pages, is of inestimable value to anyone interested in human rights.

It contains a large number of documents both national and international, including the relevant provisions of the United Nations Charter. It is because this excellent collection is available that more documents have not been appended to this book.

When the "Fridays at 10 Series" on human rights was being arranged, it was anticipated that the lectures might eventually be suitable for publication. While they were being delivered, there also emerged the idea of introducing a course on human rights at the postgraduate level. Although there was already an undergraduate course on human rights given at the London School of Economics, there was no teaching of the subject at the postgraduate level in the University of London and it was receiving little attention at other universities in the United Kingdom. Notice had been called to this situation as a result of an inquiry on the teaching of the subject being carried out under the auspices of UNESCO by the René Cassin Foundation and the International Law Association.

During the early part of 1971, a draft syllabus on human rights was prepared for an optional course for the degree of Master of Laws in the University of London. This received the approval of the Senate in time for the introduction of the course at King's College and University College during the 1971–72 session.

An examination of the sources for the purposes of the new course showed that there was no satisfactory readable introduction to the study of human rights available for students. Therefore, it was decided to publish the lectures given at King's College in the autumn of 1970 in the form of a small book. It was intended that this should serve as a short but stimulating and informative introduction to the study of this important subject.

The basic pattern of the lectures and the new London LL.M. course on human rights is the same. They involve the examination of the nature of human rights in a legal and political context as well as their substance and the means of protection. The approach is a broad philosophical one which involves consideration of human rights – collectively and individually – in a setting of political theory. Some attempt is made to present an overall integrated picture which shows some of the highlights of principle as well as the details of regulation and protection.

Ideally, any study of the subject of human rights should start with the Greek philosophers – with the writings of Plato and

Aristotle. Plato's concept of the nature and role of justice in society, its relation to the nature of man, is as relevant in the context of the treatment of the individual now as it was in the days of the Greek city state. The development of theories about law and the State from the time of Plato and Aristotle has a direct bearing both on modern political theory and on the respect for his dignity acknowledged by the State as the right of every individual.

Whether in a short series of lectures or in a degree course primarily of a legal character, it is impossible to cover the ground involved in such an approach; compromise is unavoidable. In such circumstances, compromise also has to be to some extent arbitrary. Accordingly, it was decided to take a discussion of Christianity and political theory since the Reformation as an introduction to the examination of the rights of man in the modern state. This is the ground covered by the first three lectures that have been reproduced in the first three chapters of this book. The transition from theory through a discussion of man and the modern state led naturally to consideration of certain of the more fundamental specific human rights. One would naturally, at this point, speak about two basic principles. These are the principle of non-discrimination and the principle of self-determination. In fact, the series of lectures did include one on non-discrimination but, unfortunately, the text of the lecture was not made available for publication. As regards self-determination, it did not prove possible to find a suitable speaker. There is thus a serious gap in the material contained in the book on these two basic principles. It so happened, however, that in December 1971 Lord Caradon delivered the Commemoration Oration at King's College, London, on "Race, Poverty and Population". Although this lecture does not deal with the principle of non-discrimination as such it is so relevant to that subject and so incisive and provocative that it was decided to include it in this publication to fill, to some extent, the gap left by the absence of the lecture on non-discrimination.

For the rest the lectures dealt with certain rights and freedoms, namely freedom of association, the right to work, the right to live and the right to be free. This does not, of course, cover the whole range of human rights but it does suffice to give some indication of the nature, content and limitation of these particular rights and their role in modern political society. In addition to an examination of theory and certain specific rights it was also essential to have a lecture on the legal protection of human rights and another on human rights in time of war. These are included as the last two chapters of this book.

It will be seen that the above outline corresponds to the chapters numbered 1–8 in the Table of Contents. This leaves uncovered a number of political, economic, social and cultural rights, the scope and nature of which can readily be ascertained from Dr Brownlie's *Basic Documents on Human Rights*. But it does seem necessary here to make some attempt, however brief, to fill the gap as regards the principles of non-discrimination and self-determination.

Non-discrimination

There is a widespread tendency to regard the principle of non-discrimination as elementary, basic, self-evident and universally binding, but a moment's reflection raises serious questions as to the legal nature of the principle or the existence of a general right to be treated without discrimination. There are clearly circumstances in which differences in treatment are permissible – even necessary. Few people, for example, would maintain that men and women should be treated with exact equality in all respects without regard to the differences in their natural functions. In other words, even where discrimination is not permissible in principle, it is necessary to consider what is "discrimination" and, accordingly, in what circumstances distinctions may be permitted. This does not necessarily detract from the legal character of the rights falling under the principle of non-discrimination, but it raises questions as to their exact content and effect.

If one examines the problem historically, what is now regarded as the basic principle of non-discrimination has not always been so self-evident. In fact, discrimination on various grounds has been a characteristic of law and government throughout history. Whether one considers the prevalence of slavery in the Roman Empire, the caste system in India or discrimination on grounds of race and religion in Europe until very recent times, it is clear that the principle of non-discrimination has not, in the past, been accepted as axiomatic.

If one looks at some of the earlier instruments such as the French Declaration of the Rights of Man 1789, and what is popularly called the American Bill of Rights 1791, consisting of ten amendments to the United States Constitution, there is no clear statement of the principle. The nearest one comes to such a statement is in Article I of the French Declaration, according to which men are born and remain free and equal in respect of rights. There is no doubt here a groping towards a statement of the principle of non-discrimination but the doctrine of the enjoyment of equal rights is somewhat weakened by the assertion that social distinctions are to be based on public utility.

In the case of the United States, there is an implicit recognition of the principle of non-discrimination in the Fourteenth Amendment to the Constitution which provides that no state shall deny to any person within its jurisdiction equal protection of the laws. This, however, confirms non-discrimination within a comparatively narrow field. The Fifteenth Amendment, which is clearer in its statement of the principle, deals only with the right to vote. It says that this shall not be denied or abridged by the United States or any state "on grounds of race, color, or previous condition of servitude".

These provisions in the French Declaration and Amendments to the United States Constitution may be contrasted with the explicit statements in the Charter of the United Nations. Here the concept of the dignity and worth of the human person and the equal rights of men and women are confirmed in the preamble and reaffirmed in the text of the Charter itself. Article I, paragraph 3, expressly lays down as one of the purposes of the United Nations to achieve international co-operation in promoting and encouraging respect for human rights and for fundamental freedoms for all without distinction as to race, sex, language or religion. This purpose is reaffirmed in Article 55, which provides that the United Nations shall promote, *inter alia*, universal respect and observance of human rights and fundamental freedoms for all without distinction as to race, sex, language or religion. Here one finds an explicit statement of the principle of non-discrimination in very broad terms. It is largely from the Charter of the United Nations that the modern recognition of the general applicability of the principle has developed. But even in the Charter the principle is by no means all-embracing. It is limited in the first place to the respect for and observance of human rights and fundamental freedoms and does not extend to general equality as such. Furthermore, the grounds on which distinction is excluded are stated as being "race, sex, language or religion". Thus grounds for distinction or discrimination on other bases (e.g. nationality) are regarded as permissible. This raises an interesting problem because it seems to imply that there may be human rights and fundamental freedoms which are not necessarily enjoyed on an equal basis by all people. This tends to throw some doubt on the essential legal character of the principle of non-discrimination. It should, however, be said that, unlike the principle of self-determination, whatever qualifications there may be on the right not to be discriminated against, it is a right which is capable of being enjoyed by individuals and of being maintained for their benefit against their State or government. Nevertheless, the question may still be asked whether the right as such exists in international law or by virtue of the law of nature as one binding on governments or whether it is a principle which, in order to have legal effect, requires to be embodied in international treaties or in constitutions. This is not the place to try to offer an answer to this fundamental question, but the question is one that merits careful thought in relation to the basic principle of non-discrimination and to the whole series of what are called human rights and fundamental freedoms.

Article 1 of the Universal Declaration of Human Rights 1948 affirms that all human beings are born equal "in dignity and rights". The principle of non-discrimination is spelt out in Article 2. Again it is related to the rights and freedoms set forth in the Declaration, but the Article says that everyone is entitled to the rights and freedoms "without distinction of any kind, such as race, colour, sex, language, religion, political or other opinion, national or social origin, property, birth or other status". These grounds are obviously more extensive than those mentioned in Articles 1 and 55 of the United Nations Charter. In the sense that grounds for distinction seem to be irrelevant, Article 7 of the Universal Declaration is even more broadly based. It asserts that all are equal before the law and are entitled without any discrimination to equal protection of the law. Article 2 of the Universal Declaration is reflected in Article 14 of the European Convention of 1950, which requires the rights and freedoms set forth in that Convention to be secured without discrimination on any of the grounds mentioned. It will be noted that the expression "such as" implies that the list is not exhaustive. The general principle is also reiterated in Article 2 of each of the two International Covenants of 1966.

Several instruments have been adopted to deal with discrimination on particular grounds. For example, there is the International Convention on the Elimination of all Forms of Racial Discrimination 1966, the Declaration on Elimination of Discrimination against Women 1967 and the Draft Convention on the Elimination of all Forms of Religious Intolerance 1967. Of all forms of discrimination, the one that is probably the most widely abhorred is racial discrimination. It is, therefore, interesting to see the scope of the right as defined in the 1966 Convention. The term "racial discrimination" is given a wide meaning. It is defined to mean "any distinction, exclusion, restriction or preference based on race, colour, descent, or national or ethnic origin which has the purpose or effect of nullifying or impairing the recognition, enjoyment or exercise on an equal footing of human rights and fundamental freedoms . . .". Nevertheless, the possibility of distinction applicable between citizens and non-citizens is preserved and there is a provision which authorises special measures taken solely for the purpose of furthering the interests of racial or ethnic groups or individuals. But even this saving clause is of a limited and transitional character.

It may be said that the tendency of international instruments since 1945 has been to make the principle of non-discrimination progressively stronger and more absolute. In line with this development many countries have adopted measures designed to curb or terminate racial discrimination. Yet, it may be questioned whether the creation and maintenance of good race relations can best be brought about by legal protection – whether internationally or nationally. There are those who believe that the effect of bringing race problems to a legal issue by legislation is likely to crystallise the bitterness that it is intended to destroy. Whatever may be the legal character of the principle of non-discrimination and whatever content may be given to that principle by international and national regulation, ultimately good race relations must rest on the goodwill of the peoples concerned. This again is a factor which needs to be borne in mind when one is considering the legal character of the right to non-discrimination.

Self-determination
The nature of the right or principle of self-determination has been a matter of great controversy in the United Nations Organisation.

The Charter acknowledges the principle in Articles 1 (2) and 55. In both places what is mentioned is "the principle of equal rights and self-determination of peoples". The principle is not expressly mentioned or reaffirmed in either Chapter XI or XII dealing with non-self-governing territories and the international trusteeship system; although both chapters are designed, no doubt, to give effect to the principle by the process of the achievement of self-government and independence.

No guidance is given by the Charter as to whether the principle constitutes a legal right or is political in character. Nor is there any real guidance as to its intended content. Nevertheless, ever since 1945 in the organs of the United Nations there have been pressures to strengthen and develop the principle of self-determination. It is, therefore, surprising that the Universal Declaration of Human Rights contains so little on this point, although there is a reflection of the principle in Article 21, paragraph 3. This provides that the will of the people shall be the basis of the authority of government. The Article is concerned with elections and universal suffrage. This provision in the Universal Declaration raises in acute form the question of the true nature of the principle of self-determination. In the United Nations Charter, and in particular in the provisions on non-self-governing territories and trusteeship, it appears to be concerned with the "right" of dependent territories to independence. From Article 21 of the Universal Declaration one might deduce that the principle is concerned with the political "right" of peoples to determine their own form of government.

In the Declaration on the Granting of Independence to Colonial Countries and Peoples adopted by the United Nations General Assembly in 1960, one finds a different twist. In paragraph 2, it is asserted that all peoples have "the right to self-determination". In the context, the right would seem to refer to the right of dependent territories to independence, but it is also asserted that by virtue of that right they "freely pursue their economic, social and cultural development". Paragraph 6 of this Declaration touches another note which may also be regarded as an aspect of the principle of self-determination. It affirms the doctrine of non-interference in the internal affairs of states and respect for the sovereign rights of all peoples and their territorial integrity.

In other contexts, the right of self-determination has been relied upon as justifying the claim of comparatively small groups in a state to determine their own local political organisation, or to secede either peacefully or by use of force. In the case of non-self-governing territories it is not, as a rule, difficult to identify the peoples and the territory who may claim to exercise self-determination. In other words, in that case it may be comparatively easy to decide who is entitled to the benefit of the "right". In all other cases, it is likely to be extremely difficult, if not impossible, to determine who is the person who bears the "right". This difficulty throws great doubt on the legal character of the principle of self-determination. This is a problem which is worthy of much deeper analysis than is possible in this short Introduction.

In spite of the apparent logical difficulties, the principle has been expressed as a right in Article 1 of both the United Nations International Covenants of 1966, in which the language of paragraph 2 of the Declaration on the Granting of Independence to Colonial Countries and Peoples is repeated virtually without change. What is the exact legal significance of such treaty provisions it is difficult to say, although once more in both covenants the "right" is clearly recognised as being applicable to non-self-governing and trust territories.

Bibliography

The Bibliography at the end of this book is selective, not exhaustive. It is designed to help the student to pursue his studies systematically and intelligently. In the case of works on political theory no indication has been given of the publishers or the edition because most of the works are available in numerous editions by various publishers. So long as the original text is consulted, it does not matter which edition is used. Before referring to the original, however, it is advisable to seek guidance from some secondary source, such as the appropriate chapter of Sabine: *History of Political Theory*. In the field of political theory, the most important concepts to examine are "justice", "natural law", "sovereignty" and "the State".

The list of the "classics" ends with Bentham. This is not because the later writers are unimportant, but because at this stage one begins to enter the diversity of modern thinking. Selection becomes invidious. Accordingly, the reader is referred back to the later chapters of Sabine and he may make his own choice from the sources mentioned there.

In the case of the books under headings other than "Political Theory", the publisher is given but not the edition. As a rule, it is advisable to consult the latest edition.

No attempt has been made to list articles in legal and other periodicals. Many useful articles may be found in the *British Year Book of International Law*, the *International and Comparative Law Quarterly*, the *American Journal of International Law*, and elsewhere.

The Editor would like to express his deep gratitude to the very distinguished contributors for making this book possible. He wishes to thank them both for giving the lectures in the first place and for their willing co-operation in the preparation of the text. He would also like to thank his secretary, Mrs Sylvia Seeley, for her great help in checking the proofs and making the final text ready for publication.

Finally, it should be noted that, while the credit for any merit in this book and responsibility for the views expressed belong to the contributors, the blame for any technical shortcomings must fall on the Editor.

1. Christianity and Human Rights

© THE REV. CANON SYDNEY HALL EVANS

I

It's one thing

"To sport with Amaryllis in the shade
Or with the tangles of Neaera's hair":

it's quite another thing to comb out the tangles or to bring Amaryllis into the light of day!

It's one thing to say that I am the son of my parents: it's quite another thing to attempt after 55 years to distinguish between those characteristics which I have inherited from my father and those I have inherited from my mother. Christians may have a powerful intuitive sense that there is a close correspondence between Christianity and those statements about human dignity which were formulated in the Universal Declaration of Human Rights adopted by the United Nations in Paris on 10 December 1948. But what in fact is this correspondence? The historian's task is never more difficult than when he seeks to disentangle the various strands which make up over the centuries any of the basic moral insights which have become embodied in conventions and laws. It may well be that when Amaryllis is brought out of the shade into broad daylight she may be found less attractive than she seemed to be when the lights were dimmed! So many ideas from so many different sources have been fed into our western culture that it ill behoves the Christian to claim too much or the secular-humanist to concede too little.

As one historian has written:[1] "Historians have often spoken in general terms of the far-reaching effects of Christianity in changing man's conceptions with regard to the character, the purpose and the ruling principles of human society, and no doubt the influence of Christianity upon these has been profound and far-reaching, but we think that if we are to arrive at any just and well-grounded

[1] R. W. and A. J. Carlyle, *History of Mediaeval Political Theory in the West*, Vol. 1, p. 81.

1

judgement upon this question we must be at pains to discriminate very carefully between those elements of the theory of Christian writers which are really original to them, and those in which they do but reproduce the opinions already current in the civilised world."

To begin a talk on *Christianity and Human Rights* with a quotation from one of the earlier poems of John Milton may not after all be inappropriate when one remembers the later writing of this famous Londoner. Addressing the Lords and Commons of England in 1644 in his *Areopagitica* Milton attacks their recent order "that no book . . . shall henceforth be printed unless the same be approved and licensed by such . . . as shall be thereto appointed". In this attack on censorship and this plea for liberty of the press Milton appealed to the fact that in contradistinction to the government of the day, Moses, David, St Paul and the Fathers, by precept or example, enjoin freedom in the pursuit of learning. The *Areopagitica* ends with an exhortation to the Lords and Commons of England to consider "what nation it is whereof ye are and whereof ye are the governors: a nation not slow or dull, but of a quick, ingenious and piercing spirit". He compares it to an "eagle mewing its mighty youth" and urges that it should not be shackled or restricted. "Give me liberty to know, to utter and to argue freely, according to conscience, above all liberties."

Who today can evaluate with any precision the influence of the publication of such writing as this on the subsequent thinking of western men on the issues of freedom of speech and publication, and the need of the individual for some degree of legal protection if he is to be able to act as a free man? Even if I were competent as an historian to attempt to evaluate historically the contribution towards modern declarations of human rights of ideas originating in the Christian understanding of man's nature and destiny, I would not expect to be able to draw up a detailed analysis and assessment. All I can hope to do, therefore, is to point to evidence of Christian influences affecting the movement of men's thoughts in this direction, and to attempt some general evaluation of the Declaration in the light of what I take to be the distinctively Christian understanding of ourselves as beings whose "being" is of necessity a "being-with-others".

II

What then is the human situation which makes the attempt to draw up a Declaration of Human Rights a proper, not to say a necessary and urgent need for us as human beings? I cannot set the problem before you more clearly and interestingly than has been done in a lecture given at Cambridge by Michael Howard, formerly Professor of War Studies at King's College. His theme on that occasion was "Morality and Force in International Politics".[2] I quote therefore somewhat extensively:

An ethical teaching which takes it for granted that individuals will have an orderly social background against which to work out their destinies and to make moral decisions is, however coherent and valid in itself, incomplete. Further, an ethical teaching which deals only with problems which confront an individual who has no personal and immediate responsibility for the lives and welfare of others is also incomplete. Men and women do not usually exist as solitary individuals unless they artificially create the conditions to do so by a deliberate withdrawal from society. They are normally responsible for the welfare of a social group, if only that of their immediate family; and in order to exercise that responsibility they must possess, or obtain, the necessary power. By "power" I mean the ability to organise the relevant elements of the external world so as to lead and make it possible for his dependants to lead – to use an evocative if indefinite expression – the Good Life; a life in which he is free to shape his own character by making moral decisions.

The greater the responsibility, the greater the power needed to exercise it. Responsibility will extend beyond the family to government of institutions – schools, colleges, corporations, unions, shops, offices, industries – upwards to the executive organ of society, the State itself: that complex of officials with whom final responsibility rests for ensuring that laws are made and enforced which reflect the ethical standards of the community; protecting the good man in his virtuous activity, discouraging the backslider from behaviour offensive or harmful to the rest of society, in general keeping the peace. A good community will be one whose laws a good man will wish to obey – in which he can, without offence to his conscience, be a law-abiding citizen. That postulates a law to abide by, and a

[2] D. M. Mackinnon, editor, *Making Moral Decisions* (SPCK), pp. 77–9.

power to ensure that everyone abides by it. Such a community is one where, at the very least, a man can feed his children without stealing, can protect his family without killing, and can make a living without lying to conceal his beliefs. Under conditions of tyranny, anarchy, and certain kinds of class oppression, moral behaviour of this kind can be self-defeating; in order to retain the power to exercise his responsibilities, a responsible man may have to take decisions which, judged by the standards of individual ethics, would be counted immoral. It is the function of the State to create conditions in which such terms as "crime" and "justice" make sense; in which the Good Life is possible, not only for the solitary saint, but for the ordinary man with wife and children to support; in which he is not faced with the harsh alternatives of being either a hero or a coward.

This is the justification for the absolute claim which the State makes on its citizens. This is also, as I understand it, the reason why the Christian Church, in almost all of its manifestations, has acquiesced in this claim at least since the days of St Augustine; why it has recognised, sometimes rather ruefully, the necessity of the secular arm to the physical and even the moral welfare of its members. As has been frequently pointed out, the State is a *condition* of ethical values: it provides the circumstances in which ethical activity can be carried on at all.

On this reading of our human situation two issues are emphasised: one is the desirability of what is called the Good Life; the other is the practical task of so ordering actual societies that necessary space, security and freedom are provided to enable men and women to explore and enjoy the Good Life.

By selecting this concept of the Good Life, Michael Howard both raises our expectations above current literature which concentrates on man as a "naked ape" in the "human zoo", and also reminds us of the pre-Christian origins of this concept. To the best of my knowledge this expression the "Good Life" occurs first in Aristotle, whose writings on *Ethics* and *Politics* were an early and brilliant application of a fine intelligence and sensitivity to these issues. Another tributary feeding the river of ideas and conventions which has flowed into our European culture and life is that associated with the writings and style of life of the Stoics. Those of us who in youth were introduced to that considerable old Roman, Marcus Tullius Cicero, will remember how in the

Republic he set forth the doctrine of the law of nature which had been elaborated by the Stoics. In various forms from Cicero to Locke this concept of *natural law* has been discussed by jurists and philosophers. A doctrine of *ius naturale* passed from the Roman jurists into the thinking of the Christian Church in the West and was important in the theological writings of Thomas Aquinas. The chief vehicle for the transmission of this Stoic concept into the thought of modern Europe by means of the Church was the *Corpus Iuris Civilis*, completed in the year 534 A.D. by a body of Byzantine lawyers who had been ordered to undertake the task by the Emperor Justinian. As has been well said: "It was through her law that Rome reconquered the provinces she had lost on the battlefield."

There is no doubt at all that modern declarations of human rights – building on earlier declarations like that of the American *Declaration of Independence* of 1766 and the *Déclaration des Droits de l'Homme et du Citoyen* adopted by the French National Assembly on 26 August 1789, not to mention the *Bill of Rights* 1688 and *Magna Carta* of 1215 – are not only linked historically with these earlier expressions of humanity's continuing effort to get relationships in society tolerable and tolerably just, they are also linked with this whole way of thinking about man in society for which the misleading, unsatisfactory but persistent expression is *Natural Law*. Like the concept of *Original Sin*, the concept of *Natural Law* attempts to express a deep human intuition, but does so in terms that confuse rather than clarify. *Original Sin* stands as an expression for something which is neither "sin" in the common meaning of that word, nor is it noticeably "original" in the usual sense of that term! We cannot fail to sympathise with David Hume when he wrote of the expression *Natural Law*: "the word *natural* is commonly taken in so many senses, and is of so loose a signification, that it seems vain to dispute whether justice be natural or not." Similarly the word "law" is used of positive or statute law enacted by Parliament: it is used to describe an observed uniformity of physical nature such as the so-called "second law of thermodynamics": it is used here to speak of a kind of ideal of human relationships to be the standard by which legislators should test the actual laws they promulgate. Dr A. P. d'Entrèves, in his study of this persistent concept of natural law, concludes:[3] "The notion

[3] A. P. d'Entrèves, *Natural Law* (Hutchinson), p. 116.

of natural law partakes at the same time of a legal and of a moral character. Perhaps the best description of natural law is that it provides a name for a point of intersection between law and morals."

Must we not equally locate the Universal Declaration of Human Rights in this borderland between law and morals? It sets out a concept of the kind of "space" which must be provided by the legislation of actual states if their citizens are to be sufficiently free to develop their true humanity and to live whatever kind of life it is that is indicated by the phrase "the Good Life".

If d'Entrèves has re-examined the concept of natural law from the point of view of legal philosophy, Professor John Macquarrie has more recently re-explored the concept from the point of view of moral theology. In different language he arrives at the same kind of conclusion as d'Entrèves.[4] He writes: "The expression 'natural law' refers to the norm of responsible conduct and suggests a kind of fundamental guideline or criterion that comes before all rules or particular formulations of law." He argues that one simple consideration indicates that most people do seem to believe in something like natural law. "There is no human law, not even that promulgated by the highest authority, about which someone may not complain that it is unjust. There seems to be found among most people the conviction that there is a criterion, beyond the rules and conventions of human societies, by which these may be judged." During the course of two thousand years various attempts have been made to be more precise about the details of this criterion that is behind all actual laws. Thomas Aquinas formulated the first precept of the natural law in extremely general terms: "Good is to be done and promoted, and evil is to be avoided." But every such attempt is relative and conditioned by the social and cultural environment of a particular age. This is as true of the Hebrew *Ten Commandments* as of the *Declaration* which gave a theoretical rationale to the French Revolution. Sir David Ross has listed some half-dozen *prima facie* duties: duties of fidelity, reparation, gratitude, justice, beneficence, self-improvement and the duty of not injuring others. Ross argues that there is a kind of fundamental moral knowledge given with human existence itself.

This so-called natural law is not therefore capable of precise formulation. It exists within our western tradition as a kind of

[4] John Macquarrie, *Three Issues in Ethics* (SCM Press), pp. 82–110.

intuition, a kind of vision of what ought to be, a touchstone for describing the justice or morality of actual laws and rules. The constancy of this criterion is therefore "not that of a law but of a direction". We are talking about "a constant tendency, a kind of inbuilt directedness, a pointer within us which orients us to the goal of human existence". Patrick Nowell-Smith claims that the more we study actual moral codes of different nations and cultures we find that these do not differ in major principles. "All have the same direction, as it were", writes Macquarrie; "they aim at the development of a fuller, richer, more personal manhood, and to this extent they are in accord with and give expression to the natural law."

The fact that the Declaration of Human Rights was agreed to in 1948 by so wide a variety of men of differing cultures and creeds is surely a further indicator to the truth of this ancient and persistent human intuition that there is an "unwritten law" which safeguards the truest needs of humanity in accordance with which actual laws either assist or prevent the movement of men towards fuller existence.

Sometimes attempts to give expression to the content of this fundamental intuition have been made academically in the study by moralists, jurists or theologians. Sometimes they have been hammered out in the heat of political upheaval. But always they express this basic human hope, this basic human vision in which men reach beyond themselves towards a better life for man in society: a reaching out which expresses a concern both for the better ordering of society and for the good life of individual persons within society.

III

This intuition of which we have been thinking, this idea of natural law, antedates the Christ-event; but the Christ-event and all the thinking about man and society that has issued from the Christ-event within the Christian community has reinforced this intuition and has given more precise content to the ideal. What is distinctive about the Christian ethic is not its fundamental principles: these are shared by serious-minded persons of different traditions. What is distinctive, to quote Macquarrie again, is the special context within which the moral life is perceived: "This special context includes the normative place assigned to Jesus Christ and his teaching, not indeed as a paradigm for external imitation but rather as the criterion and inspiration for a style of life." The special context includes also the moral teaching of the Bible and its interpretations; the practices of prayer and worship, and community membership of a fellowship sustained by faith and hope.

Without in any way seeking to diminish the contribution of Christian thinkers and theologians to the development of what we may call human-rights thinking, shall we not be getting the emphasis more nearly correct if we say that the most distinctive contribution of Christianity has been what I would call the Christ-presence, the embodying in an actual person who died for his convictions rather than compromise for his personal safety, of these dimly discerned ancient human aspirations and hopes to which the concept of natural law points? Is it not the fact of the actual embodiment in the particularity of an historical person of the concept of what it really means to be a human person which has enabled Christianity to evoke responses in other human beings of similar attitudes and commitments? Has it not been the distinctive achievement of the whole Christian continuum that it has enabled an abstract concept and hope to be actually interiorised in this person and that? By means of the Gospel men and women have been brought to an understanding and practice of what is truly and authentically personal, inspired by the life, teaching and death of Jesus and the effect of his dying on other men and women down the ages. Christian martyrs have witnessed by accepting death rather than compromise to the reality of those truths about human nature and destiny which were embodied in a special manifestation in Jesus whom men came to acknowledge as Christ.

That this may be the right way to relate Christianity to human-rights thinking is reinforced for me by an observation of the present Dean of Christ Church, Dr Henry Chadwick. Writing of the patristic theologican Origen he says:[5] "The Gospel brings to actuality what is present in men potentially and its 'newness' consists of the concrete example of Christ himself." "The Gospel is the republication of the law of nature implanted by Creation. It does not bring a new morality, but a recognition of the divine righteousness and love as the underlying ground of the highest ethical aspiration."

[5] Henry Chadwick, *Early Christian Thought and the Classical Tradition* (OUP), p. 105.

IV

If then the main contribution of Christianity towards the growth of the concept of human rights has been the presence of innumerable men and women who have responded to the style and claim of Christ and thereby have raised human standards and the quality of human relationships, can we isolate more precisely one or two influences emanating from this Christian faith and style of life? I suggest two which historically have been of great and widespread importance – the *attitude to children* and the *attitude to women*.

I doubt if there is very much written evidence to which we can appeal for support in making the claim that a changed attitude towards children, their welfare and upbringing, has come about as a result of the Christian symbol of the Madonna and Child and the Gospel story of Jesus with the children. But no one can underestimate this influence. "They brought young children for him to touch; and the disciples scolded them for it. But when Jesus saw this he was indignant and said to them, 'Let the children come to me; do not try to stop them; for the kingdom of God belongs to such as these. I tell you, whoever does not accept the kingdom of God like a child will never enter it.' And he put his arms round them, laid his hands on them and blessed them." This blessing of the children together with the introduction of infant baptism into the practices of the Church have, I suggest, down the centuries greatly affected the attitudes of adults towards children and the growth of a particular style of family life.

We are on firmer ground when we explore the effect of Christianity on the status of women. W. E. H. Lecky, in his famous, if now little known two-volume *History of European Morals from Augustus to Charlemagne* (published 1869), was no devotee of Christianity. But for all his astringent criticisms of the failure of the Church to embody the moral standards for which it stood, Lecky devotes the final chapter to an extended study of "The Position of Women" and regards Christianity as the main influence for changing their position.[6] He writes: "A very important result of the new religion was to raise to a far greater honour than they had previously possessed the qualities in which women peculiarly excel." He singles out a number of Christian

[6] W. E. H. Lecky, *History of European Morals from Augustus to Charlemagne* (Longmans Green), Vol. II, Chapter V, pp. 358–70.

women who had great influence on their sons and husbands. "It may be truly said," writes Lecky, "that women's instinct and genius of charity had never before the dawn of Christianity obtained full scope for action. . . . There has been no period, however corrupt, there has been no Church however superstitious, that has not been adorned by many Christian women devoting their entire lives to assuaging the suffering of men; and the mission of charity thus instituted has not been more efficacious in diminishing the sum of human wretchedness, than in promoting the moral dignity of those by whom it was conducted." "Whatever may be thought of its theological propriety, there can be little doubt that the Catholic reverence for the Virgin has done much to elevate and purify the ideal of woman and to soften the manners of man." "In the Sisters of Charity the religious orders of Catholicism have produced one of the most perfect of all the types of womanhood."

There is more of this kind of comment to be found in Lecky, and if we allow ourselves to reflect on the influence of women as wives and mothers, then what is said about the liberating effect of Christianity on women suggests here again a hidden, unspectacular but fundamental area of life in which Christianity has helped forward man's understanding of himself and of the dignity of the individual which lies behind such a Declaration of Human Rights as we are considering.

If we can argue that in respect of women and children early Christian thinking was in advance of that of the contemporary world, a more ambiguous area is that of Christian thinking about *slavery*.

As twentieth-century men and women we have to keep reminding ourselves not to expect of men and women living in the third or fourth centuries attitudes that are commonplace to ourselves. Everybody is imprisoned within the thought-forms and value-judgements of his own age, and only a few far-seeing persons in any age are able to change these value-judgements even ever so little. Christians no less than pagans were children of their time. Many ideas which you find in Christian writers are the current ideas of the society of those times; and there are Christian insights which gradually bring about a change of attitude. In learning how to disentangle and discriminate we are indebted to historians who can bring a high level of objectivity to their task. Such are R. W. and A. J. Carlyle in their six-volume *History of Mediaeval Political Theory in the West*.

In Part III of Volume I they discuss the political theory of the New Testament and Fathers.[7] Paul, as we remember, speaks in *Romans* of the Gentiles who do by nature the things of the law though having no written law like the Jews, but are, as he says, a law unto themselves in that they show the work of the law written in their hearts. This is analogous to Cicero's idea of a natural law, written in men's hearts, recognised by men's reason, distinct both from the positive law of the State and from what Paul recognised as the revealed law of God.

Jesus had taught that in the eyes of God the distinctions between Jew and Gentile were neither fundamental nor permanent, and we know how Paul formulated his doctrine of equality: "There is no such thing as Jew and Greek, slave and freeman, male and female: for you are all one person in Christ Jesus" (*Gal.* 3: 28). Carlyle's comment is: "The Christian Church set out on its history with a conception of human nature which had outgrown the sense of national limitations, a conception which coincided very closely with the conception of the contemporary philosophy."

What then of the attitude of Paul and the Fathers to slavery? Paul is more concerned with a man finding interior freedom than exterior freedom. He is more concerned to help slaves to come to terms with their condition than to change that condition. To be a slave or freeman, he says, makes no difference to God. Both are equally capable of knowing God and of living as children of God. The slave is possessed of reason and capable of virtue. His Letter to Philemon illustrates two principles: slavery is not in Paul's mind unlawful: slavery as a condition is only external and has no existence in the moral and spiritual life. In relation to Christ it is a matter of indifference whether a man is a slave or a free man. But by this same token Christian masters must treat their slaves with fairness (see *Colossians* 3: 22–4: 1), for the master is no dearer to God than is the slave. This same attitude which emphasises equality but does not require a change in the social institution is to be found in the Fathers generally. They are equally concerned to secure fair treatment of slaves by masters. Slavery then is regarded as just one among many misfortunes that may befall a man, such as the loss of a limb. What matters is that the slave be free in his inner self. Like St Augustine, the Church generally accepted slavery as necessary under the actual circumstances of

[7] R. W. and A. J. Carlyle, *ibid.*, Vol. I, Pt. III.

society, but pressed on masters the duty of treating slaves with consideration and kindness.

It could therefore be argued that in this instance Christianity was an influence retarding the development of human-rights thinking by accepting the institution of slavery while teaching the slave that he was no less in the eyes of God than his master. It could also be argued that what Christianity was all the time teaching about the essential equality of all men in the eyes of God was in the long run more influential in securing external freedom than would have been a narrowing of interest to the abolition of the institution of slavery itself. Nor must we forget that what is called slavery in the ancient world was in experience often little worse than domestic service in large households in the nineteenth century. It needed the abuse of slavery and the transport of captured Africans to the Americas to arouse in Christian consciences a recognition that here was a traffic in humanity of a quite different sort from that of which Paul and the Fathers were writing.

V

We must now turn more specifically, but briefly, to consider Christianity as itself an institution caught up in the politics of life. Every idea if it is to gain currency has in some way to be institutionalised. But it is the tragedy of institutions that they tend to sap the vitality of the original idea. The Christian idea became institutionalised, and for several hundred years, at least from Charlemagne to the Renaissance, the Christian Church in the West became something of an international state containing within it smaller nation-states. Once Christianity became embodied in the institutional forms of the mediaeval Church, Churchmen as statesmen were caught up in the tragic predicament of all statesmen, the inevitability of the power-game with its equally inevitable compromises and use of force.

Opponents of Christianity most often seize on this period and aspect of Christianity and think that when they have called attention to the Inquisition they have said all they need to say in order to dismiss the Christian claims. Nor should Christians have any hesitation in admitting that terrible things have been said and done by members of the Church in the course of history. But it was from within this same Church that there arose in the course of time a Francis, a John Hus, a Martin Luther, a Thomas More, a Teresa, a Damien, a Shaftesbury, an Elizabeth Fry, a Pope John. *Ecclesia semper reformanda.* The Church carries always within itself a judgement on its own aberrations: the Christ-presence breaks through in the person of this saint and that reformer and a return to God liberates new life.

There is a sense in which part of the battle for human rights has been fought out over the centuries within the Church itself, not least in the working out today within the Church of Rome of the new thinking displayed at the Second Vatican Council. Something of a revolution took place within the debate on Religious Freedom leading to the publication of *The Declaration on Religious Freedom* – a declaration on the right of the person and of communities to social and civil freedom in matters religious. This is a vast and fascinating exercise towards greater integrity, and I dare hardly touch on it briefly for fear of distorting by over-simplification. The issue has a long history. Various papal utterances on the rights of the individual have led to some development in the notion of religious freedom also. But it was John XXIII's *Pacem in Terris* which really made possible the radical change of outlook expressed in the Declaration of Vatican II.

The Declaration begins by calling attention to two preoccupations of contemporary man: "a sense of the dignity of the human person" and the need for "constitutional limits . . . to the powers of Government". The desire of man for freedom, freedom to develop responsibly as persons in society, and the corresponding desire for limitation on the powers of government are singled out among the aspirations of modern man and declared to be "greatly in accord with truth and justice". In relation to actual practice in certain areas of the world in which the Roman Church has been a dominant influence, and in the light of earlier, vaguer statements concerning the matter, nothing but welcome can be given to the statement in the Declaration: "This Vatican Council declares that the human person has a right to religious freedom." This freedom is defined as "immunity from coercion" by individuals or societies in religious matters. Religious liberty is presented as a human right and not as a concession to *force majeure*.[8]

It will take time for the full implications of this Vatican

---

[8] Enda Mcdonagh, *The Declaration on Religious Freedom of Vatican Council II* (Darton, Longman and Todd).

Declaration to be studied, assimilated and translated into changed attitudes and practices, but here at least in principle and in intention is a major change of mind and heart on the part of one of the largest of the Christian communities in a direction which will not only support the Declaration on Human Rights but actually lead to legal and political changes in this direction.

VI

I must bring these widely ranging observations to a close and leave it to my successors in this series of lectures to expound the *Declaration on Human Rights* in the social and political context of our times.

If *Magna Carta* was one step towards political maturity and the *Bill of Rights* another in our own country, what is presented to us in the *Declaration on Human Rights* is a statement of universal range embracing all men everywhere regardless of country, colour or creed. It is a spelling out for an entire world in the language of lawyers and statesmen of what is implicit in Paul's declaration of human equality nearly two thousand years ago.

But the spelling out of the concept of human rights and the consequent limitation of power contains within itself an assumption about the true nature of man and about man's need to be protected against himself. The Declaration expresses both an awareness of human dignity and of the threat man is to himself. Pollution of the environment is a contemporary example. The assertion of human rights therefore is not just an exercise in philosophical reflection: it is intended as political action. A state must needs limit its own power if it is to guarantee the rights of the individual to freedom. But we must not blind ourselves to the fact that rights-of-man thinking does not easily attain this authoritative position in the minds of statesmen and politicians. Human-rights talk is always in danger of becoming little more than an ornamental or ideological flourish. Declarations of this kind have to be formulated in very general terms. To make a difference to human life these general concepts have to be translated into actual laws. If human rights are to be of any use they must be effective rights and not just ideals. Mere assertions of human rights do not guarantee men against the abuse of power. Man cannot get away from what he is. He undermines and overthrows the very institutions he has himself set up as guarantees. Civilisation is as brittle as egg-shell.

Christianity has never been blind to this human perverseness and need for conversion. A Christian will inevitably therefore experience some feelings of unease when the talk is of human *rights*. Talk of rights is lawyers' language, not the language of theologians. Theologians talk of love and of love as a duty. Love can be spoken of as a duty because in Christian understanding it means a chosen attitude. The language of Christ is the language of love and duty. "Thou shalt love thy neighbour as thyself", and the parable of the samaritan and the man who was robbed and left dying by the roadside has fixed this teaching for ever in an incomparable and forever evocative story. The Christian language about human relationships focuses on *the other* as the object of duties rather than on the self as the subject of rights.

But translate theological language into such approximate categories as are meaningful in the social and legal sphere and you have to use the language of justice as the balancing of rights. The concept of the human person as the subject of rights and object of duties takes us nearer the Christian language than talk of human rights alone does.

The Christian, then, in his concern for the neighbour, must put his full support in the social and political realm behind the *Declaration on Human Rights*; but his greater concern will be to bring men and women to such an inner attitude of mind and orientation of feeling that their ideals can be embodied in laws and customs, translated from aspirations into actualities.

This calls not only for education but for conversion – a radical change of heart until a man learns to forget himself in concentration upon the true well-being of the other.

2. The Rights of Man since the Reformation: An Historical Survey

© PROFESSOR J. H. BURNS

My subject has the Reformation for its *terminus a quo*; and I therefore feel no need to apologise for beginning my treatment of it with the religious dimension of the concept of human rights. I feel the less need, speaking as I do under the auspices, in part, of the Faculty of Theology, and in a series inaugurated a week ago by the Dean in a lecture which put the matter very firmly where I am sure it ought to be put: in the context of Christianity and the role of Christianity in western civilisation. This does not mean that I feel no hesitation in speaking in such a dimension. My hesitation is all the greater because I come to this place from the godless college in Gower Street and now stand, I suppose, more or less half way between Smithfield on the one hand and Tyburn on the other. As it happens, I am also speaking only a few days before the canonisation in St Peter's of the forty English and Welsh martyrs – a subject, variously, of controversy and of gratification. I do not refer to these matters solely in the vein of academic persi-flage – the equivalent, in my case, of following the advice given to Alice: "Curtsey while you're thinking what to say." These subjects, the sinister associations to the east and west of us at this point in London, and the ceremony soon to take place in Rome, have a distinct relevance to the theme of these lectures. It was true, surely of the Protestants who died at Smithfield, it was true of my fellow-Papists who died at Tyburn, it was true of my fellow-Scots who died in the seventeenth century in defence of the Covenant, that, however much they differed, they were all in some sense giving their lives for a kind of spiritual integrity. They all died for the right of conscience; and I want to suggest in this lecture that it is with the concepts of spiritual integrity and the right of conscience that this subject, historically, begins and ends.

We must not get this point into the wrong perspective. Mani-festly, none of the groups of people I have just mentioned –

16

admirable as they doubtless were – could be classed as liberals of any kind or as having any specially tolerant attitude in matters of religious faith. Sixteenth-century society, whatever else it was, was not a "permissive society". Whether it was better or worse for this may be debatable, but it was clearly not, save in certain isolated and transient instances, permissive or tolerant. Neither then nor for most of the seventeenth century were most people prepared to consider the possibility of toleration. But the society which lived through the Reformation and Counter-Reformation had been confronted with a challenge to established authority which had at its heart the Lutheran concept of Christian liberty. It is easy to see, and commonly and rightly said, that liberty of any kind was one of the more obvious casualties of the struggles that followed Luther's protest in 1517. Yet it is also true that the whole movement we call the Reformation and all the controversy it precipitated would revolve around the conviction that at the heart of the Christian religion lies a concept of freedom which can be lost sight of only at the cost of the integrity of Christian faith itself. This is why the harsh and bitter conflicts which led to the horrors of Smithfield and Tyburn are so important for the history of freedom and of human rights.

Moreover, the nature of these conflicts was such that groups of Christians repeatedly found themselves compelled to assert and claim a right to disobey, a right to resist in certain cases what would otherwise have been for all Christians in that age the legitimate commands of the established authorities. For all Christians these authorities were ordained by God; and the conflicts of the period, both in their origins and in their development, were apt to face men and women with a choice between the normal duty of obedience and the upholding of their own conceptions of religious truth, their own integrity as Christians. To choose the latter might mean claiming a right to *dis*obey, a right to dissent; and it need hardly be underlined that these claims were essential and basic to the evolution of the concept of human rights as we have known it in modern Europe.

To this one important rider may be added at the cost of abandoning for a moment the chronological order which I wish in general to preserve. The point seems appropriate here because it follows so directly from the religious dimension in which I have begun these remarks. Many years ago now, the late A. D. Lindsay pointed out in his uncompleted work on *The Modern Democratic State* that the development of Puritan religious thought in seventeenth-century England had as one of its consequences the clear and distinctive emergence of the idea that law, in so far as law was concerned to protect rights, provided a framework within which the free life of the spirit, the life of grace, might be led; and that this was the only legitimate business of the law in this connection. Here, it seems to me, are two aspects of a central theme in the evolution of ideas about government, law, and rights in the historical period with which we are dealing. There is, on the one hand, the idea that the business of government is essential but limited, that government has a necessary function to perform, but that it has no legitimate claim to an omnicompetent control over the human mind. On the other hand there is the associated idea that in this limited business government should be concerned above all to uphold certain rights so that, within this guaranteed framework, men may freely live their lives as independent spiritual beings. Now, however much has changed in the life of the individual and of society in the past three hundred years, however much we may have lost the religious convictions of the sixteenth and seventeenth centuries, I suggest that there still remains at the heart of much of our thinking in these matters the conviction that the business of law and of government is this kind of business. It is not, that is to say, the business of government or of law to provide an all-inclusive ordering of men's lives. This is in a sense to deny that the purpose of the state is, as both Plato and Aristotle had maintained, to promote "the good life". The fulfilment and completion of life are not within the competence of political society as such. If this is a limited and negative view of government, the point of the limits and the negations is not to narrow and confine human life in society, but on the contrary to liberate men's lives as much as possible from legal discipline and control, provided only, but always, that a certain minimum of order can be secured, within which the life of freedom can be led.

In returning, as I must now briefly do, to the sixteenth century, I want to direct attention to what might be termed the more narrowly political aspects of a movement of thought which has so far been considered mainly in its spiritual and moral dimensions. John Neville Figgis, who brought to the history of political ideas one of the subtlest minds of his generation, said of the sixteenth century and its sequel that "political liberty was the residuary legatee of ecclesiastical animosities". His argument was that the ecclesiastical divisions stemming from the Reformation produced a situation in which the otherwise absolute power of the state could be and was effectively challenged, at least in some places and for certain periods, by a concept of the state in which constitutional liberty and political rights could exist and flourish. The state, that is to say, had, in these cases, lost any position from which it could claim to exert a single, undivided, centralised control over society and the individual. Now this view, if it is valid, must be important for our subject. Political liberty, after all, is apt to be in or near the forefront of our minds when, in modern times, we talk of human rights. At the same time it is, I think, important to notice how gradual, hesitant and even ambiguous is the emergence of liberty in this sense in the period with which I have so far been largely concerned.

If one encounters the notion of liberty in the sixteenth century it is most likely, upon close scrutiny, to reveal itself as consisting in *a* liberty. The word in this sense has a plural form, and indeed the plural form "liberties" is much more important in this period than the single abstract notion of "liberty". This is because the concept is being used in a situation where those who support a dissenting religious position are politically concerned much more to protect and enhance the liberties or privileges of the order or class or corporate group to which they belong than to advocate or foster any general concept of liberty which would apply to all members of society. Thus the supporters of, especially, those Protestant movements which found themselves at odds with persistently Catholic governments – in France, for instance, or in Scotland – were, in some important respects, seeking to entrench more deeply the vested rights they enjoyed in virtue of a certain position within the social structure. If it is, as I believe, a solecism to deny the reality and sincerity of the religious motivation in these groups, it would none the less be naïve to ignore the reality of their other motives – the social, economic and political goals which could be pursued so often under the banner of traditional and immemorial "liberties".

For this reason it is difficult, perhaps impossible, to find in the sixteenth century any notable writer who would regard the people, the *populus* with whose ordering and organisation both religion and

politics were concerned, as synonymous with the whole population, or even the whole adult population, or even the whole adult
male population of society. It was a limited and hierarchically
structured group that men of that age envisaged when they
thought of a commonwealth or political society. Even John Knox,
in whom there is so much that has the tang of democracy (if we
must use that ambiguous and slippery word), was led – was
indeed compelled, in his own view, by circumstances – to distinguish between "the people assembled together in the body of a
commonwealth" – the organised political society – and "the rascal
multitude" – the mob, the many-headed beast which had (Knox
claimed) been responsible for the image-breaking and pillaging of
churches which followed his vehement preaching in Perth, Stirling,
and Edinburgh. And what is true of Knox is true *a fortiori* of less
radical and impassioned writers and orators in an age when there
was indeed concern for liberties, but not (as I understand the
matter) as yet much concern for civil or political liberty in general.

If, again, little has been said directly of *rights* as such in the
sixteenth century, this is simply because the term is not one that
plays a large part in the literature of the period. And when the
term is used, it tends to be used in contexts where its reference
is much less likely to be to the rights of the subject than to the
right or authority or title of those who govern him. Thus Theodore
Beza writes *Du droit des magistrats*, George Buchanan *De jure regni
apud Scotos*; and both are indeed concerned to advocate *limits* to
the right or authority enjoyed by the magistrate or by the crown.
By implication, then, these writers are doubtless attributing certain
rights to the people, either collectively or as individuals. But they
do not write directly in terms of such rights against the authority
of the state. They think first of the rights of the crown or of the
magistrate, and then seek ways in which these rights can be
limited for the protection of the community against misgovernment.

Only gradually, in the course of the seventeenth century, does
the particularised notion of rights as the privileges or liberties of
specific orders or groups within society develop into a broader
and more generalised concept to which we may begin to attach the
term "liberty", and in regard to which we can use phrases like
"natural rights", "human rights" or "the rights of man". The
gradual nature of the change and the very deliberate speed with
which it came about are well illustrated by English experience in

the seventeenth century. Even in the constitutional conflicts of the mid-century decades the assertions of rights tend to be concerned with rights that are alleged to be rooted and grounded in the traditional constitutional structure of the realm of England. They are specifically the rights of Englishmen at large, and not simply, as they would have been in the past, the rights or liberties enjoyed or claimed by particular corporate groups of Englishmen. Yet they are still the rights of Englishmen, not yet the rights of man. The Petition of Right, to take one of the earliest documents in this group, is not concerned with any abstract or general notion of rights which belong to men as such. It is concerned with particular and extremely specific rights which had allegedly been violated by the policies of Charles I and his ministers. And even in relation to the concept "the rights of Englishmen" one has to ask the difficult question, "How far does the notion of an Englishman, of a member of the English commonwealth, in fact extend at this period?" It may be arguable that that notion did not effectively reach lower in the social scale than the level of the patriarchal heads of families who perhaps constituted even for Locke near the end of the century the effective political community with whose rights and liberties he was concerned in his *Two Treatises of Government*. Even if this is so, however, it remains true, I think, that the idea of rights, even within the context of English constitutional argument and political controversy, was being both sharpened and extended.

In a wider context there was being developed during the seventeenth century a framework for a still more liberal and comprehensive theory of rights. I have in mind here the immensely important development of the doctrine of natural law. I must not attempt what would be impossible here without distortion – an investigation of the complex question how far and in what sense the seventeenth century saw the birth of what has been called the modern concept of natural law. All I need emphasise is this. In a period when what would now be the work of political scientists, of sociologists, and of social psychologists was done above all by jurists, the most influential jurisprudence was the jurisprudence of the great natural-law school of Grotius, Pufendorf, and their many followers. It was from the works of these jurists that educated Europeans throughout the seventeenth and eighteenth centuries took most, if not all, of their systematic ideas about society and

government. And the aspect of what they found which is fundamental to my present concern is this: they found the majestic and
confident assertion of the objective existence and universal
authority of a body of rational principles of conduct and judgment.
These principles are rational in that they can be established in-
controvertibly by a process of reasoning in which any ordinarily
intelligent man can share. The common reason of mankind, then,
will establish, verify, authenticate these principles. And it must
be noted that, without being in any sense atheists or even agnostics
in matters of religion, the jurists of the natural-law school from
Grotius onwards claimed to be advocating principles of which
the authority and truth were independent of the validity of any
particular religious position, independent indeed, in principle,
even of the existence of God. We must notice too that this concept
of rational order was expressed deliberately and unequivocally in
terms of *law*. This readily afforded a framework for a doctrine of
natural rights; for it was natural enough for those who thought
or were educated in juristic or legal terms to argue that, just as any
particular system of civil law necessarily generated corresponding
civil rights, so the system of natural law which is universally valid
generates natural rights which can be universally claimed by all
men.

Now it would be quite false and misleading to suggest that the
immediate consequence of the authoritative establishment of the
principles of natural law was to generate everywhere a correlative
notion of natural rights. This was not the case. The impact and
consequences of natural-law thinking varied widely, and Rousseau
was only one of those who pointed out that the doctrines of
Grotius and Pufendorf could be and had been used to uphold
absolute power in the state and thus, in Rousseau's view, to deny
man's essential liberty. Other thinkers used the same doctrines to
build up and advocate a theory of natural rights aimed at safeguarding and fostering the freedom of the individual. The story
is not a simple one; and to understand even that part of it which
most concerns us we still have to identify the forces which were
at work in the seventeenth and eighteenth centuries to ensure the
emergence of the idea of natural rights from the theory of natural
law.

The English, and subsequently the American, variation on
natural-law thinking is critically important here, and I must there-

fore return to seventeenth-century England and in particular to John Locke. Locke is one of those thinkers who are perhaps characteristically English (and I speak as a Scotsman) in that they are undogmatic, eclectic, ready to see both sides of a question, and perhaps to hold both sides of a position at once. Locke does at all events seem to represent a kind of amalgam of many, if not all, of the strands I have so far tried to identify in this lecture. In Locke (and in others whom I have passed over unmentioned) you can see the continuing influence, mediated to him through Richard Hooker, of concepts of law and society which achieved perhaps their most impressive statement in the *Summa Theologiae* of St Thomas Aquinas. In Locke, too, can be seen the reflected light of the great Anglican solution to the problems of religious authority and of the relationship between that authority and the individual – the light that shines through the pages of Hooker's *Laws of Ecclesiastical Polity*. But in Locke there also reverberates that Puritan concern which I have mentioned already – concern for the rights and integrity of conscience and for the essential importance of preserving a channel for the free life of grace which cannot be provided by any human authority. Locke's *Letters concerning Toleration* are as important for an understanding of his political theory as are the *Two Treatises of Government*. For our purposes their importance can hardly be exaggerated, reminding us as they do that the theory of natural rights in Locke is not only concerned with the rights of property and of political liberty – it is explicitly concerned with the rights of conscience, with rights that are manifested in freedom of belief, freedom of religious practice, freedom of worship, in all ways that do not trench upon the rights of others so as to require the intervention of the civil power. For Locke as for many mid-century Puritans before him, the church is a voluntary association of men who come together to enjoy communion with God and with one another according to their own understanding of religious truth. The natural rights of man include the right of every individual to seek his own salvation in his own way.

It was not, of course, only in this religious dimension that Locke's ideas were, as I have suggested, seminal for the later development of the belief in human rights. Locke also took up from Hooker the notion of consent. He took up the developing concept of the liberty or liberties of Englishmen. He fused these into a doctrine in which men, rational by nature and free because they are rational, are capable of knowing for themselves the fundamental principles or laws by which their conduct ought to be governed. All they need is the additional force and authority of civil government to ensure that these principles will be respected by all, not only by those who are prepared to respect them for their own sake. Men thus enjoy under the law of nature natural rights which are inherently theirs as men, and which constitute a standard prior to all government and indeed to all society, by which society and government can be judged. These rights are, in sum, the rights to life, liberty, and estate. Man has the right to live, to live freely, and to live of his own. The last point has been, for recent students and critics of Locke, at once a stumbling-block and a fascinating historical problem. What exactly did Locke understand by the right to estate, and how, precisely, did he think that right was related to the authority of government and society? These are questions which it would be tedious and pedantic to seek to explore in the present context. All I need do here is to point out that in Locke's *Two Treatises of Government* you have the kernel of what was to become the classic form of the doctrine of natural rights. It was to be classic not only for England and for continental Europe (for Locke soon became one of the presiding geniuses of the eighteenth-century Englightenment). Perhaps still more important, the doctrine was to become classic in North America, where the English colonists made of this doctrine one of the essential elements in the revolutionary ideology with which they entered the struggle with the government of George III.

In using, perhaps loosely, the term "ideology", I do not want to engage in the complex argument about its proper interpretation. I want only to draw attention to what might he called an extension of the range of the idea of rights as we move from the seventeenth into the eighteenth century. The fact that we encounter the doctrine in a document like the American Declaration of Independence with its assertion of the existence of "unalienable rights", among which are "life, liberty, and the pursuit of happiness"; the fact that we find it again, still more elaborately, in the French Declaration of the Rights of Man and the Citizen in 1789 – these facts indicate that the idea of rights is now being brought fully into the arena of actual political conflict and action, that it is crystallising into something like a political programme. I believe that this crystallisation has been permanent, and I shall be arguing later that, despite intellectual developments that have undermined its theoretical respectability, the crystallised doctrine of natural rights has retained its vitality at some of the most fundamental levels of political and social thought and feeling both in Europe and in all those parts of the world where European influence has been significant or decisive. At this stage I want only to recall and to signalise the most important single statement of the doctrine – most important in the sense of having almost beyond question been far more widely read than anything I have so far mentioned. I mean *The Rights of Man* by Tom Paine, written in 1791 as a reply to Edmund Burke's attack on the French Revolution, its principles, and its English partisans. Paine demonstrated in this book that the doctrine enshrined in the pages of Locke and of many other writers in the eighteenth century could be expressed in a most effective popular form and could be made a vehicle of radical democratic thought to a degree that could not have been anticipated when Locke wrote his *Treatises of Government* for the nascent Whig oligarchy of late seventeenth-century England. But Paine also showed, especially in the second part of the book, that the doctrine could be developed and expanded in directions which Locke and his contemporaries could scarcely have imagined or understood. This development took the rights of man from the simple "bourgeois" bases of life, liberty and property into the realm of such rights as we would now associate with the services and safeguards provided by the welfare state. From the basic individualist doctrine there now emerges a concept of the framework of security and well-being which society ought always to provide for its members – and these members now emphatically included the humblest and poorest in the land. It must be clear to us all that this has been one of the most important developments in the doctrine of rights in our own time. One need only look at some of the more recent documents in the long series of declarations of rights to see how this broadening of the area in which, it is claimed, society should guarantee and protect rights has altered the character of these declarations.

Yet, powerful and popular as this doctrine was to be in the years after the publication of Tom Paine's *Rights of Man*, powerful and popular as it still is, the fact remains that, philosophically, the doctrine has from the eighteenth century onwards been subjected to a series of radical and damaging criticisms. All I can do here is to indicate where these attacks come from and what their general character has been and to suggest the not unfamiliar conclusion in the history of ideas, that political controversy of this kind makes strange bedfellows, so that arguments which start from very different premises may finish up in very much the same position. The common position in this case is the decisive rejection of any concept of inherent individual rights belonging to men as such.

Why did the doctrine of natural rights suffer this undermining process? It was in part a result of the whole movement of sceptical and secularist thought in the eighteenth century, which sapped the religious foundations of the doctrine. The hold that the doctrine had on people's minds owed so much to the acceptance of these religious assumptions that to question them effectively was to weaken that hold at once. And of course nothing was more radically questioned by the thinkers who make up the movement we call the Enlightenment than precisely these assumptions and beliefs. Within that general point there lies a more specific one. The scepticism of a writer like David Hume is directed very much against the possibility of holding any such concept as natural law, and therefore, of course, the related belief in natural rights. To this must be added the empirical and cautious scepticism of a mind like that of Edmund Burke, alarmed at the implicit dangers of a doctrine which challenges established institutions by appealing to an abstract and general criterion. There is, further, in a vein in some ways similar, though in the end very different in direction and effect, the profound scepticism and hostility of Jeremy Bentham and the whole utilitarian school which followed him. The utilitarians argued that the appeal to natural rights was at once useless and dangerous. It was useless because it sought to substitute abstract metaphysical argument for the measurable, quantitative criterion of the greatest happiness of the greatest number. And it was dangerous because it carried the anarchic implication that any institution, whatever its general effect on the well-being of society, might be open to challenge and attack and overthrow by those who claimed that it infringed their inalienable natural rights. It is on these grounds that Bentham attacks the doctrine of natural rights in the work ultimately published as *Anarchical Fallacies*, but earlier submitted (unsuccessfully) for publication in the *Anti-Jacobin* under the still more revealing title *Pestilential Nonsense Unmasked*.

So the sceptics had their say and their day, whether their scepticisms were expressed in the dispassionate tones of Hume, the impassioned and indignant tones of Burke, or in the style of those who, like the Benthamites, believed that a scientific technique for achieving human happiness could and must be substituted for the irrelevant rhetoric of natural law and the rights of man. But the sceptics were not the only, nor perhaps in the end the most effective critics of the theory of individual rights. Some of its sceptical critics at least shared the individualism of its proponents; but it was just this basic assumption of the theory that was to be attacked and rejected by a new and powerful school of social and moral philosophy in the nineteenth century.

There are traces, indeed, of some such view as this in Burke, some inchoate idea of the community itself as something which we cannot properly understand as if it were a mere device or contrivance fashioned from individuals by individuals for the fulfilment of individual goals. The new view – which is, as is so often the case, an old view revived: in this case the view of society we find in Plato and Aristotle – the new view can be seen hesitatingly and ambiguously in Rousseau. It can be seen quite unhesitatingly and, if obscurely, certainly without ambiguity, in Hegel and in those nineteenth-century thinkers who derive from Hegel. In this view, the reality and significance of the human individual are subordinated to the greater reality and significance of human society. It is not necessary to hold that these doctrines must have sinister "totalitarian" consequences or must be prejudicial to the well-being or even, in some sense, the freedom of the individual. What is clear is that these doctrines emphatically reassert what Rousseau had said – that "the social order is a sacred right and the source of every other right". It is from society, it is in and through the concrete relationships of an actual society that men derive the rights they have. It is indeed only within that social context that it can make any sense to talk of rights at all.

A celebrated essay by one of the greatest English writers of this persuasion – F. H. Bradley – bears the title "My Station and its Duties"; and it is perhaps true to say that there is in the thought of the Hegelian or Idealist school a salutary corrective emphasis upon duties as opposed to rights – on man's obligation to the society in which he lives as the primary element in his relationship to it. Yet this does not mean that these thinkers are not concerned with rights and with freedom. Their argument is indeed that the self-realisation which is the truest kind of freedom can come only through living in a society where duties and rights are correlative aspects of an integral situation in which neither individual nor community can be understood in abstraction from one another. In Thomas Hill Green, for instance, one finds an acutely sensitive liberal conscience, a profound awareness of the necessary conditions for the free development of the individual. Yet it must remain true in the end for Green, as for all whose thought runs along the lines that run back through Hegel to Rousseau, that the concept of a right against society, of a right which is not intrinsically connected with the social structure which creates and protects it, is self-contradictory. Such rights have and can have no real or concrete existence: they are non-entities.

This kind of intellectual development, moreover, is taking place during a period when the effective ideologies that are coming to dominate political life are increasingly ideologies of the group, not of the individual. For these ideologies it is the nation or the race or the people or the class that constitutes the vital focus of politics. Thus we encounter in the nineteenth and twentieth centuries the phenomenon of nationalism – deeply concerned for rights and for liberty, but concerned above all for the rights and freedom of the collective body of the nation. Not many years ago, the late Tom Mboya, when asked about the problem of freedom in newly independent Kenya, said explicitly that when they talked of freedom they had in mind essentially the freedom of the Kenyan people as whole, as a collective entity. Now the significance of this view must not be discounted; nor should we undervalue its positive usefulness as a solvent of what would otherwise no doubt have been rigid and oppressive imperial systems. Yet the fact remains that in theories like this the older notion of rights may easily be overshadowed or overwhelmed. Take another example – the kind of theory which holds that the proletariat is the necessary vehicle of human progress from capitalism to socialism. People who hold such a view may be suspicious of and hostile to the whole way of thinking with which the notion of rights has been associated. Lenin, for instance, devoted a pamphlet explicitly to *The Deception of the People by the Slogans of Freedom and Equality*. But if they could be induced to say anything about rights in a positive sense they would presumably say that the only rights that matter are the historically determined rights or claims of the proletariat as a class – as the ruling class of the future and the builders of the classless society which is to come.

In the climate of nationalism and socialism, with the climatic disturbances of racism and totalitarian socialism in the offing, it is far from surprising that the doctrine of individual human rights has had a rough time not only philosophically but also in the world of practical politics and ideological controversy. And yet it survives. Many people seem reluctant to surrender the belief, however fallacious the philosopers may show it to be, and however irrelevant the politicians may tell them it is, that individual human beings, simply because they *are* human, have claims to make upon and against society which any decent and civilised society ought to meet. Even the theory of natural law itself, so long exposed to the blasts of criticism from legal positivists and others, has had a revival of a kind in the traumatic circumstances which prevailed during and after the Second World War. There was, it seems to me, a widespread feeling that monstrous things had happened and were happening, things of which the monstrosity consisted above all in the violation of the rights and the integrity of the human personality. To seek, in this situation, for some notion of law which should transcend the positive law of the state – that positive law which had so often been manipulated for tyrannical purposes – to seek for a law which might afford a basis for essential human rights was a readily understandable quest. It was a quest which led both to a revival of natural-law thinking and to a renewed belief in the importance of asserting and declaring the rights of man.

This is a phenomenon which occurs again and again in the late 1940s and 1950s. It is evident in the impressive declaration of rights embodied in the constitution of the Indian Republic. It is reflected in the expanded Declaration of the Rights of Man and the Citizen which formed part of the constitution of the Fourth Republic in France. A little later we have the European Convention on Human Rights seeking to establish actual machinery for the vindication of the rights declared in common by its signatories. Now inevitably the detailed contents of these and other similar documents reflect a very different social order, a very different concept of society and of what individuals are entitled to demand of it, from those which prevailed in the classic period of the doctrine of human rights with which the central passages of this lecture were concerned. Yet again and again you will encounter the unmistakable echo of phrases which are first clearly heard in the natural-rights doctrines of the seventeenth and eighteenth centuries. All the philosophical arguments and all the ideological pressures have failed to extinguish the stubbornly persistent belief in "certain unalienable rights".

I want to end by referring to a curious episode which is perhaps a kind of parable. Some years ago, but well within the period since the Second World War to which I have just been referring, it was reported that among the equipment of a West African witch-doctor there had been found, besides the usual fetishes, a copy of Tom Paine's *Rights of Man*. I mention this in no spirit of derision or contempt for the fetishist. No one who lives in a society like ours can with decency take a high line about fetishism: there are posters on the Underground – to mention only one illustration – which represent a form of fetishism that is neither obscure nor exalted. But the fact I have cited seems to me to have serious and interesting implications. It would seem to mean that, at a time when the political ideas of the West were generating the forces of African nationalism, it was somehow felt that Paine's book embodied a power that could be harnessed, a magic, if you like, to be added to the forms of magic which Africa already knew. Now we may feel confident enough that books do not have this kind of magical power. But a book like this, which must have been read by many thousands times the number of people who read any other book I have mentioned, must surely have in it some power of a very special kind. Could it after all be true that Paine's book and the doctrine which it enshrined and developed do embody permanent and essential elements in the concept of a free and just society? To answer affirmatively may be to reach a grossly unhistorical conclusion at the end of what was offered as an historical survey; but it may well be, for all that, the most important reflection which such a survey should provoke.

3. Man and the Modern State

© PROFESSOR RENÉ CASSIN

A. French Text

Dans le cadre des huit conférences organisées par le King's College sur les Droits de l'Homme pour l'automne 1970, un sujet m'a été assigné "l'Homme et l'Etat moderne".

Ce sujet est tellement vaste qu'il comporterait s'il devait être traité sous tous ses aspects, un cycle entier de conférences (lectures). Heureusement, sa portée est limitée si l'on tient compte, d'une part, que d'importants droits de l'homme (droit à la vie, à la liberté corporelle, au droit au travail, liberté d'association) sont traités dans des conférences distinctes et d'autre part que nous aurons à nous occuper spécialement de deux libertés: la liberté d'expression et de réunion (freedom of speech and of assembly).

Or il s'agit de deux libertés qui depuis *longtemps* – bien avant les droits au travail ou à l'éducation – occupent dans la liste des droits de l'homme une place importante et même pour l'une capitale. Elles ont été sans difficulté l'objet, dans la Déclaration universelle adoptée en 1948 par l'Assemblée générale des Nations-Unies, d'une reconnaissance spécifique formelle dans les articles 19 et 20.

Le plan de notre exposé est donc tout tracé. Nous devrons en premier lieu examiner assez longuement les transformations générales réalisées dans les rôles respectifs de l'individu, de l'Etat et des autres groupes sociaux, depuis l'époque libérale où se sont affirmées les premières libertés classiques. Cet examen ne portera pas seulement sur l'origine scientifique, sociale et politique de ces transformations, mais aussi sur leurs conséquences concernant la liste et le contenu des droits et libertés reconnues.

Il nous sera plus facile ensuite d'examiner l'influence particulière que ces transformations ont exercé sur la portée pratique et les conditions d'exercice, d'abord de la liberté d'expression et ensuite de celle de réunion.

C'est un lieu commun que de souligner les considérables changements réalisés depuis la fin du XIXe siècle dans la conception des
droits de l'homme dans les pays libéraux qui, comme l'Angleterre
et la France et même à certains égards les Etats-Unis, ont été
les premiers à affirmer, soit dans des déclarations (comme celles
de 1689, 1778, 1789) soit dans des lois, l'autonomie juridique de
l'individu face au monarque ou, plus récemment, à l'Etat. Alors
que le XIXe siècle avait été en grande partie consacré à consolider,
élargir et garantir ces libertés dans l'Etat officiellement gardien de
ces libertés, la notion de liberté constitutive d'un droit-faculté a
peu à peu changé de caractère et s'est, sinon partout, du moins en
un nombre croissant de domaines, complétée de droits-prestations.
La voie était ainsi ouverte à accueillir comme droits de l'homme
des aspirations d'ordre culturel (droit à l'éducation) ou économique
et social (protection du travailleur, sécurité sociale, etc.) com-
portant très souvent une prétention à certaines prestations positives
de la part de la collectivité. Ainsi s'est dégagée peu à peu la notion
nouvelle du *Welfare State*. Les attributions de l'Etat se sont accrues
d'une manière prodigieuse, surtout à la faveur des deux guerres
mondiales. Après le retour à la paix, beaucoup de ces attributions
ont subsisté au moins partiellement, même dans les pays libéraux
vainqueurs, *a fortiori* dans les Etats vaincus incapables de revenir
à un régime libéral.

Cette orientation, déjà perceptible dans les constitutions de
l'Amérique latine, s'est précisée de plus en plus dans les Etats
européens démocratiques, République allemande comprise, à
partir de la Révolution russe de 1917. La création de l'O.I.T. et
l'adoption consécutive de nombreuses conventions du travail ont
été à leur tour le point de départ de nouveaux progrès dans
l'égalité, compensée par le recul de certaines libertés, comme celle
du commerce et du contrat.

Mais cette évolution, originairement due aux découvertes
scientifiques et techniques qui ont transformé les conditions de la
production économique et des communications entre les hommes,
a été accompagnée de deux phénomènes qui, selon les meilleurs
juges, ont exercé une influence directe d'une ampleur et d'une
portée considérable.

En premier lieu entre l'individu et l'Etat se sont interposés des
groupes sociaux nouveaux très différents des groupes classiques,
territoriaux ou spirituels traditionnels: à savoir les syndicats

patronaux et ouvriers, les groupes professionnels financiers industriels, agricoles, commerciaux, les trusts d'édition, d'information, de presse. Le droit de *groupe*, la notion de *masse* ont pris une importance imprévue et ont contribué à déformer la structure et les conditions d'exercice des droits traditionnellement reconnus.

Il n'est que de se référer aux changements profonds qui se sont opérés dans la notion de propriété et dans le droit des contrats. Les contrats collectifs se sont multipliés d'abord en Angleterre, puis en France. La notion de coopération a pris une extension considérable. Sous ce premier aspect, les droits purement liés à la personne humaine, sans disparaître, ont pris des aspects extérieurs nouveaux et ont vu naître à côté d'eux des droits collectifs.

L'apparition des grandes institutions internationales – formes premières de l'organisation juridique de la communauté humaine ou, au moins, d'une pluralité d'Etats – constitue le second phénomène. Alors que, sur le plan intérieur, les attributions de l'administration croissaient et continuent à croître sans arrêt depuis 50 ans, on assiste à un phénomène d'internationalisation de plus en plus fort dans nombre de domaines. La vieille Union postale universelle a été longtemps seule, ainsi que l'union continentale des chemins de fer européens. A l'heure actuelle, tous les moyens de transports des personnes, des marchandises et surtout des idées, aviation, navigation, radiodiffusion, télévision, font l'objet d'accords internationaux. Le monde est devenu plus petit. Il faut insister sur ces deux éléments de plus en plus importants dans les structures mondiales.

(A) D'une part l'être humain a de plus en plus, sa vie conditionnée par les exigences de la vie collective. Matériellement il est en rapports continus de dépendance vis-à-vis de l'Etat.

C'est un fait facile à contrôler tous les jours. Mais, par réaction de défense, l'homme moyen dont le niveau de vie s'est accru, devient de plus en plus exigeant sur le terrain du respect de sa dignité et de ses droits fondamentaux. La Déclaration universelle des Droits de l'Homme a jailli comme la protestation de tous les êtres humains, contre les attentats à la vie et à la liberté des humains qu'Hitler et Mussolini ont perpétrés en déclanchant la plus vaste contre-révolution qu'on ait connue contre les principes de liberté, d'égalité et de fraternité humains dominant le monde – contre-révolution qui a avili l'être humain et mis à néant le progrès qui avait fait par l'abolition de l'esclavage et les conventions de la Croix-Rouge.

Mais la Déclaration n'a pas été que cela. Elle a aussi placé parmi les conditions de dignité de l'homme, le droit à participer au Gouvernement du pays dont il fait partie – c'est-à-dire indirectement le droit des peuples à disposer d'eux mêmes et celui des êtres humains à manger, à s'instruire, à échapper à l'oppression et à la misère.

Plus encore: au lendemain de la deuxième guerre mondiale qui s'est achevée sur l'utilisation de la force nucléaire conquise récemment par l'homme, la collectivité humaine a éprouvé comme un moment de méfiance contre ses propres excès. Nul doute, qu'avec le recul du temps, on découvrira dans la quasi-simultanéité de la conquête de la puissance nucléaire et la promesse faite aux peuples de dresser une Charte des Droits de l'Homme obligatoire pour les Etats, beaucoup plus qu'une coïncidence chronologique, mais un lien direct de corrélation. Les hommes ont tenu à se tracer eux mêmes une ligne de conduite et à poser des barrières devant l'usage meurtrier des forces atomiques par les Etats.

Je viens de rappeler que, en 1945, on n'a pas seulement entendu formuler une Déclaration de principes très élevée, mais platonique. La Grande-Bretagne l'a parfaitement compris: elle a été la première à présenter en 1947 devant la Commission des Droits de l'Homme des Nations-Unies, un avant-projet précis de convention sur les Droits de l'Homme. Notre délégation avait perçu l'immense intérêt de cette méthode. Aussi lorsque l'idée d'une Déclaration-manifeste proposée par les Etats-Unis a triomphé provisoirement, nous avons été de ceux qui ont proclamé que la Charte des Droits de l'Homme ne serait une réalité que si la Déclaration était complétée par des Pactes d'application définissant les droits de l'homme avec précision et assortis de mesures de mise en oeuvre garantissant l'exécution ponctuelle des obligations des Etats définies par ces Pactes. On comprend très bien que, vu le nombre d'années, qui a été nécessaire pour obtenir des Membres des Nations-Unies l'adoption de Pactes (18 ans), les nations ont bien fait d'adopter dès 1948, date où la guerre froide a commencé à sévir, une Déclaration de base, nécessaire pour orienter la politique des Etats du monde, anciens ou jeunes. Mais on ne saurait trop approuver l'initiative britannique qui, au vu des difficultés révélées à New-York pour l'adoption des Pactes

universels, a transporté en Europe, les premiers articles déjà
élaborés des futurs Pactes qui ont servi de base à la convention de
sauvegarde adoptée par les membres du Conseil de l'Europe le
4 novembre 1950, avec des moyens de mise en oeuvre et des
institutions de garantie, absolument neufs et aussi efficaces que
possible entre Etats souverains.

(B) J'ai longuement traité des rapports nouveaux établis entre
l'Homme et l'Etat moderne. Il faut insister maintenant sur l'intervention nouvelle de la communauté universelle ou au moins des
groupements régionaux dans le cas où l'individu n'aura pu obtenir
de son pays par l'intermédiaire d'une justice et d'une administration bien organisées, le respect de ses droits et libertés fondamentales.

Sur le terrain des Droits de l'Homme qui est intimement lié au
maintien de la paix, on assiste en effet à un mouvement tendant à
dessaisir l'Etat de sa traditionnelle compétence domestique
exclusive. Le monde ne veut plus entendre un Hitler proclamer,
comme il l'a fait en 1933, devant la Société des Nations, son droit
exclusif de fixer sans recours le traitement de ses ressortissants.
Le monde moderne ne s'accommode pas du droit antique du père
de famille romain qui revendiquait le *jus necandi* sur son esclave et
même sur son fils.

L'affaiblissement des mesures de mise en oeuvre comprises dans
les Pactes de 1966 et, plus encore, le retard apporté pas les Etats –
sauf 9 d'entre eux – à ratifier ces Pactes sont, au premier chef, dus
à la réticence des Gouvernements. Ceux-ci, mis au pied du mur,
veulent retenir le plus longtemps possible, comme un attribut
essentiel de leur souveraineté, le droit de régir comme ils l'enten-
dent le statut de leurs ressortissants.

Or le droit secondaire, mais éminent, de contrôle de la communauté juridique universelle est la suite légitime, logique de
l'évolution plus haut décrite. A l'heure actuelle, l'homme n'est
plus seul en face de l'Etat moderne: à l'intérieur, les groupes
sociaux divers ont acquis une place impossible à anéantir. Mais,
justement, un recours extérieur est aussi né au profit de l'individu
menacé gravement dans ses droits fondamentaux. Dans l'intérêt
de sa dignité et de la paix, il y a pour lui possibilité d'en appeler
à une instance supérieure internationale. En vertu des engage-
ments pris pendant la deuxième guerre et confirmés de suite après
par les gouvernements envers les peuples, les Etats ont le devoir

d'accepter, sur ce problème capital des Droits de l'Homme, d'incliner leur souveraineté traditionnelle devant des organes impartiaux de contrôle et de censure de caractère régional ou même universel.

Si, après ces vues générales sur l'homme dans ses rapports avec l'Etat moderne, nous tournons notre attention vers deux libertés déjà reconnues par les civilisations libérales, la liberté d'expression (freedom of speech) et celle de réunion, nous pourrons constater que leur importance, surtout celle de la première s'est considérablement accrue, mais que leurs conditions d'exercice ont profondément changé et sont devenues à certains égards plus difficiles et même sérieusement menacées.

I. La *liberté d'expression* s'est surtout dégagée au XVe et XVIe siècle comme une des manifestations de la liberté de conscience ou de croyance. Mais elle a conquis assez rapidement ses caractères propres en devenant la liberté de se faire et d'exprimer une opinion. La Déclaration française de Droits de l'Homme dit que "Nul ne peut être inquiété pour ses opinions". Or la Déclaration universelle (art. 19) dit que "toute personne a droit à la liberté d'opinion et d'expression. Ce droit comprend la liberté d'avoir des opinions à l'abri d'interférence et de chercher, recevoir et diffuser des informations et des idées par tous moyens, sans égard aux frontières."

On peut dire que c'est une des libertés les plus fondamentales de l'homme, car nul n'a pouvoir de forcer sa pensée interne et ses sentiments, ni de l'empêcher d'exprimer extérieurement sa pensée et ses sentiments. D'autre part, la liberté d'objection et de discussion est une des sources les plus sûres de la vérité.

(A) Cette liberté est une de celles qui se manifeste par les moyens et sous les aspects les plus divers.

Originairement c'est la *parole*, mode d'expression primitif qui a été très tôt utilisé: la profession de foi, l'opinion politique, les discours et conversations publiques (comme à Hyde Park) ou entre amis.

Mais la liberté de la parole est utilisée à l'Eglise, en famille, dans le travail (parlements, clubs), dans les Universités (asiles de liberté), dans les Ecoles. L'étude de l'indépendance de l'enseignement et des libertés académiques est fort instructive: elle est affirmée par la Déclaration universelle et certaines déclarations figurant dans des documents de l'UNESCO.

La liberté d'expression se manifeste en second lieu, dans *l'écrit* (lettres, missives, tracts, gazettes, manuscrits), le spectacle (théâtre). Elle s'est depuis Gutenberg, manifestée par l'imprimé (léger ou lourd, journal ou livre). Le régime de la presse n'a été organisé que lentement dans les divers pays. Mais dans les pays démocratiques, il se déploie largement, à l'abri de la *censure*.

Cette liberté d'expression du journaliste se conjugue avec le droit du lecteur à s'informer. Son respect est le critère d'un régime démocratique.

L'époque récente a, par suite des découvertes scientifiques, vu s'accroître considérablement *les moyens de communication de la pensée et de l'opinion :* le télégraphe, le téléphone, le phonographe ou disque, la télegraphie sans fil, le télex, le recours au telstar sont des exemples.

La radio, le cinéma, la télévision offrent de telles facilités de communications à de multiples personnes, qu'on les appelle des *mass media.*

Quant aux écrits et imprimés, leur diffusion s'est accrue considérablement par des machines d'impression rapide, par les reproductions mécaniques des écrits et journaux : copies, photocopie, électronique. Un journal a récemment annoncé qu'au Japon on venait de trouver la reproduction électronique du journal télévisé comme du journal ordinaire. N'oublions pas le magnétophone qui est fort commode mais peut être utilisé à l'insu de celui qui parle et servir à qui veut interférer dans sa vie privée.

(B) J'ai assez décrit les changements survenus pour parler de leur influence sur les conditions d'exercice de la liberté de parole et d'expression, en apparences si simples. C'est le *caractère industriel* des modes de transmission de la pensée qui domine l'époque moderne, d'une part, les aménagements industriels sont si coûteux qu'ils deviennent hors de portée d'individus et même de groupes trop faibles. Les entreprises de presse sont obligées de se concentrer pour vivre; les petites anciennes sont mortes ou menacées. La radio, la télévision ne peuvent être exploitées que par des groupes puissants et très souvent font l'objet d'un monopole d'Etat. Malgré le texte de la Convention de sauvegarde européenne du 4 novembre 1950 qui proclame la liberté d'expression et d'exploitation de ces moyens (c'est le cas en Europe), la Commission européenne, saisie d'une réclamation, a déclaré qu'il fallait tenir compte des pratiques déjà existantes au moment où les Etates ont signé le traité.

La menace contre l'exercice de la liberté d'expression dérivant de ces pratiques ne peut être conjurée que si les offices de monopoles sont indépendants du Gouvernement ou si la composition du Conseil d'administration garantit que les différentes tendances de l'opinion, en tous sujets et notamment à l'occasion des élections politiques, peuvent équitablement se faire entendre.

Par ailleurs, la censure préalable, écartée pour la presse dans les pays, libres est devenue la règle pour les films.

La défense pratique de la liberté d'expression plus que d'aucune liberté ne peut être abandonnée à l'arbitraire de l'Administration. Il n'y a pas de matière qui exige, au même degré, des tribunaux indépendants (judiciaires ou administratifs), capables de briser les obstacles illégaux opposés à l'exercice légitime de la liberté de parole et d'expression et de refuser de prononcer des condamnations pénales injustifiées contre ceux qu'on inculpe de paroles ou écrits contraires à la sécurité publique, à la sûreté de l'Etat, à la bonne entente entre citoyens (excitations raciales).

Il faut que ce soient des juges indépendants qui apprécient les limites que doit rencontrer la liberté, même quand il y a des textes. Dans les pays autoritaires, c'est toujours en recourant à des incriminations de ce genre, que le pouvoir qui n'a pas voulu réprimer ou prévenir directement par la force, agit pour étouffer l'opposition et la liberté des écrivains.

Même dans les pays libéraux, les modes nouveaux d'expression ne sont pas entièrement soumis au même régime que la presse. Sans doute les particuliers diffamés par l'Office de télévision, peuvent exercer un recours en justice contre leurs diffamateurs. Mais le droit de réponse existant en de nombreux pays pour répondre avec pertinence aux citations et attaques de presse, n'est reconnu que dans de rares pays, face à la radio et à la télévision. D'autre part des lois sont nécessaires pour réprimer les atteintes à la vie privée qui peuvent être faites par la surveillance des paroles de chaque particulier; les écoutes téléphoniques et l'abus de magnétophones minuscules et secrets, constituent des exemples. L'ordinateur dont l'usage se répand à notre époque constitue un exemple nouveau encore plus capital de conservation et de communication, mais qui contient aussi un potentiel de menace pour l'intimité de l'individu.

II. Il semblerait que le *droit de réunion* aurait pu échapper à des changements aussi graves et importants que la liberté d'expression. Il n'en est rien.

(A) La Déclaration universelle déclare dans son article 20 que "toute personne a droit de se réunir à d'autres en assemblée pacifique et en association".

Il consacre ainsi le droit de réunion qui est une des manifestations de la liberté d'expression, de caractère collectif, mais qui se distingue de l'association par son caractère *temporaire*. La réunion a éte définie comme "constituant un groupement momentané de personnes formé en vue d'entendre l'exposé d'idées ou d'opinions ou de se concerter pour la défense d'intérêts". Le caractère provisoire est complété par l'idée d'organisation et par l'objet de la réunion.

Longtemps la réunion a fait partie des actions qui devaient être autorisées par le pouvoir. Puis est venue une phase libérale. En France c'est la loi du 30 juin 1881 qui a proclamé la réunion libre et la loi du 28 mars 1907 a dispensé les promoteurs de toute déclaration préalable. Mais celle-ci a été rétablie par l'ordonnance d'Alger du 30 novembre 1943 introduite en métropole le 9 août 1944.

La réunion a toujours fait l'objet d'une réglementation. D'une part, l'autorité investie des pouvoirs de police peut l'interdire si elle redoute que la réunion "soit de nature à troubler l'ordre public".

Les préfets peuvent même interdire toute réunion dans un ressort donné: les réunions privées peuvent même faire l'objet d'interdictions analogues.

(B) En réalité, l'évolution des moeurs vers l'intolérance constitue une grave menace pour la liberté. En effet, dès qu'une réunion est annoncée, souvent d'autres groupements se mobilisent et lancent une annonce parallèle de manière que la *menace de trouble incite l'autorité à interdire la réunion projetée*: si bien que l'intervention des autorités de police doit souvent jouer pour assurer la liberté de réunion.

En France, le Conseil d'Etat a été souvent saisi de recours en la matière: ce sont au fond les juridictions qui garantissent et la liberté et le droit de réglementation du maire et du préfet.

En Angleterre, je crois savoir que la situation est aussi délicate. Le *Riot Act* de 1769 confie à l'autorité publique de grands pouvoirs contre l'obstruction de la voie publique, comme contre la menace de trouble de l'ordre.

Le droit de réunion ne se confond pas avec les manifestations et attroupements utilisant la *voie publique*. Les cortèges, défilés, rassemblements de personnes et, d'une manière générale, les manifestations sur la voie publique, doivent, en principe, faire l'objet d'une *déclaration anticipée* s'ils sont organisés à l'avance (ce qui permet de les protéger ou de les interdire). Mais très souvent les *attroupements* se forment sans avoir été annoncés à l'avance. Ce sont eux qui donnent aux pouvoirs publics le plus de soucis. Ils sont soumis à un régime répressif.

L'évolution signalée au début de cet exposé s'est manifestée dans le domaine du droit de réunion comme en d'autres domaines. Ce n'est pas un mystère que le monde entier est secoué dans maints pays, par les réunions permanentes et les manifestations violentes de jeunes gens qui se disent hippies ou maoistes ou gauchistes. Certains se livrent à des violences et des déprédations qui ne paraissaient pas suffisamment prévenues, réprimées ou réparées par les mesures de droit commun. D'où le vote de lois particulières. En France, la loi anti-casseurs du 8 juin 1970 répond à cet objectif.

En réalité cette mesure de réaction de la Société apeurée aurait pu être très dangereuse pour les libertés de l'ensemble des citoyens, notamment les cortèges syndicaux. Heureusement le Parlement a voté en France une loi assez modérée.

Mais ce dernier épisode confirme que les libertés publiques sont toujours précaires, menacées. Dans notre société en transformation les droits de l'homme doivent être constamment protégés par le juge, soit à l'appui de l'administration quand celle-ci défend les libertés, soit contre les particuliers, contre les pouvoirs publics, si c'est eux qui menacent ou étouffent la liberté.

Cette protection accordée par le juge indépendant est si précieuse, que sur le plan international, il y a un mouvement grandissant pour confier le contrôle des agissements des Etats à des Commissions composées de personnalités compétentes et impartiales chargées de vérifier les faits, préparer des recommandations et, quelquefois, obtenir des gouvernements convaincus de violations, certaines réparations.

En dernier recours, c'est au juge international qu'il faut confier le soin de décider si un droit de l'homme a été ou non violé. Mais ne nous dissimulons pas qu'avant que le droit triomphe dans les rapports entre Etats, un long temps s'écoulera. Un combat tenace, continu doit être cependant mené sans découragement, notamment par l'éducation des jeunes générations, car il ne peut y avoir de paix si les droits de l'homme ne sont pas respectés.

B. English Text

In the course of eight lectures organised by King's College on Human Rights in the autumn of 1970, I have been assigned the subject of "Man and the Modern State".

This subject it so vast that if it were treated in all its aspects it would require a whole series of lectures to itself. Fortunately its scope is limited by virtue of the fact that some important human rights (the right to live, the right to personal liberty, the right to work and freedom of association) are the subject of separate lectures, and secondly that we are specifically concerned here with two freedoms: freedom of speech and of assembly.

We are concerned then with two freedoms which for a long time – much longer than the rights to work and to be educated – have occupied in the list of human rights an important and, so far as one of them is concerned, a pre-eminent place. They were without difficulty granted specific formal recognition in Articles 19 and 20 of the Universal Declaration of Human Rights adopted in 1948 by the United Nations General Assembly.

The plan of our discussion is thus drawn up for us. We will, in the first place, have to examine in some detail the general changes which have taken place in the roles of the individual, of the State and of other social groups respectively, since the liberal epoch in which these first classic liberties were established. This examination will not only deal with the scientific, social and political origin of these changes, but also with their consequences with regard to the number and content of the rights and liberties recognised. For the sake of convenience, we will first examine the special effect of these changes on the practical content and conditions of exercise of freedom of speech before passing on to those affecting freedom of assembly.

It is well known that considerable changes have taken place since the end of the nineteenth century in the concept of human rights in liberal countries like England and France and even in some respects the United States, countries which were the first to affirm, whether in declarations (like those of 1689, 1778, 1789), or in laws, the legal autonomy of the individual in relation to the Crown or, more recently, to the State. While the nineteenth century had been to a great extent devoted to consolidating, enlarging and guaranteeing these freedoms in a State which was officially their guardian, the notion of freedom as involving "freedom from" has gradually changed its character and is now complemented by "freedoms to", if not everywhere, then certainly in an increasing number of areas. The road was thus open for the acceptance as human rights of cultural aspirations (the right to education) or economic and social aspirations (protection of the worker, social security, etc.), involving very often a demand for a certain positive contribution on the part of society. So little by little the new notion of the Welfare State emerged. The powers of the State have grown enormously, especially as a result of the two world wars. After the return to peace, many of these powers remained, at least in part, even in the victorious liberal states, let alone in the defeated states which were unable to return to a liberal regime.

This tendency, which could already be seen in the Constitutions of Latin America, became more and more pronounced in the democratic European states, including the German Republic, after the Russian Revolution of 1917. The creation of the International Labour Organisation and the subsequent adoption of numerous Labour Conventions were, in their turn, the point of departure for further progress in equality, counterbalanced by the restriction of certain freedoms, like those of commerce and contract.

But this evolution, originally due to scientific and technical discoveries which transformed the conditions of economic production and human communication, was accompanied by two phenomena which according to the best judges, have exercised a direct influence of considerable scope and effect.

In the first place, there have come between the individual and the State new social groups very different from the classic traditional territorial or spiritual groups. I am referring to the associations of employers and workers, to the professional, financial, industrial, agricultural and commercial groups, and monopolies of publishing, information and the press. The law of the *group*, the idea of the *mass* have taken on an unexpected importance and have contributed to the distortion of the structure and conditions of exercise of the traditionally recognised rights.

It is only necessary to refer to the changes which have taken place in the idea of property and the law of contract. Collective contracts have multiplied first in England and then in France. The idea of co-operation has taken on a wider significance. This phenomenon, then, has meant that the rights which are purely related to the human personality have, without disappearing, taken on new external aspects and have been complemented by new collective rights.

The appearance of the great international institutions – the first examples of the legal organisation of the human community, or at least of a majority of states – constitutes the second phenomenon. Just as, on the internal plane, the powers of the administration have grown and continued to grow without stop for fifty years, we are witnessing a phenomenon of increasing internationalisation becoming stronger and stronger in several fields. The old Universal Postal Union was for a long time alone, just as the Continental Union of European Railways was. At the present time, all the means of transport of persons, merchandise and above all ideas – aviation, navigation, radio and television – are the subject of international agreements. The world has become smaller. It is necessary to emphasise these two increasingly important aspects of the world system.

(A) On the one hand, the life of the human being is conditioned more and more by the demands of collective life. Materially he is in a position of constant dependence on the State.

This is something which one can readily see in every-day life. But, by a sort of defence reaction, the average man whose standard of living has improved, becomes more and more demanding of respect for his dignity and his fundamental rights. The Universal Declaration of Human Rights rang out as the protest of all human beings against the outrages on human life and freedom which Hitler and Mussolini perpetrated in unleashing the greatest counter-revolution ever known against the principles of human liberty, equality and fraternity – a counter-revolution which debased the world and made it materialistic by immediately going back on the progress which had been achieved by the abolition of slavery and the conclusion of the Red Cross Conventions.

But that was not all. The Declaration included among the conditions of the dignity of man, the right to participate in the government of the country to which he belongs – that is to say, indirectly, the right of peoples to self-determination and that of human beings to eat, to be educated, and to escape oppression and misery.

Furthermore, immediately following the second world war, which had culminated in the use of nuclear power – a force recently acquired by man – the human race experienced the feeling of mistrust of its own excesses. Without doubt, in the course of time, one will discover more than a chronological coincidence, rather a direct correlation, between the fact that the conquest of nuclear power and the promise to establish a charter of the rights of man binding on all states, were almost simultaneous events. Mankind attempted to lay down a code of behaviour for itself and to place obstacles in the way of the murderous use of atomic force by states.

I have mentioned that in 1945 it was not intended merely to formulate a lofty but ineffectual declaration of principles. Great Britain understood this perfectly; she was the first to present in 1947, before the United Nations Commission on Human Rights, a detailed plan of a convention on human rights. The French delegation appreciated the great advantages of such a method. So, while the idea of a declaration manifesto proposed by the United States triumphed for the time being, we were among those who declared that the Charter of Human Rights would only be a reality if the declaration were supplemented by treaties which defined the precise way in which human rights were to be applied and which were equipped with machinery which guaranteed the punctilious execution of state obligations as defined in these treaties. I quite accept that in view of the number of years which it has taken for members of the United Nations to adopt treaties (eighteen years), states did very well to adopt in 1948, when the cold war began to intensify, a basic declaration which was necessary to give direction to the policy of states old and new. Nevertheless, one cannot praise too highly the British initiative which, in view of the difficulties revealed in New York for the adoption of universal treaties, brought about the transportation to Europe of the first articles, already elaborated, of the future treaties which have served as the basis of the convention on the protection of human rights which members of the Council of Europe adopted on 4 November 1950, equipped with the means of execution and institutions of supervision, absolutely new and as effective as is possible among sovereign states.

(B) I have dealt at some length with the new relationship established between Man and the Modern State. It is now necessary to emphasise the new intervention of the universal community or at least of regional groupings in cases where the individual would not be able to obtain from his own country, through the intermediary of well organised justice and administration, respect for his fundamental rights and liberties.

In the area of human rights, which is linked with the maintenance of peace, we are witnessing a trend towards divesting the State of its traditional *exclusive* domestic competence. The world no longer wishes to hear a Hitler proclaim, as he did in 1933 before the League of Nations, his exclusive right to determine without appeal the treatment of his nationals. The modern world no longer accepts the ancient right of the Roman father, who claimed the right of life and death over his slave and even over his son.

The weakening of the provisions of implementation contained in the treaties of 1966 and, still more, the delay of states in ratifying them – only nine have done so – is due above all to the reticence of governments. They, though driven into a corner, wish to retain for as long as possible, as an essential attribute of their sovereignty, the right to decide for themselves on the status of their nationals.

Thus the secondary but important right of supervision by the universal juridical community is the legitimate and logical outcome of the evolution which I have already described. At the present time, man is no longer alone when he faces the modern State: within the State various social groups have entrenched themselves in such a way that they cannot be displaced. But quite properly, an external means of redress has also been created for the benefit of the individual whose fundamental rights are gravely threatened. In the interests of his dignity and of peace, it is possible for him to appeal to a higher international tribunal. By virtue of the undertakings given during the second world war (and afterwards confirmed) by governments towards their people, states must agree, with respect to this fundamental problem of human rights, to modify their traditional sovereignty before impartial organs of supervision and censure, whether regional or even universal.

If, after these general views on man and his relationship with the modern State, we turn our attention towards two freedoms already recognised by liberal civilisations, freedom of speech and of assembly, we may state that their importance, above all that of the first, is well established, but that the conditions of their exercise have changed profoundly and have in certain respects become more difficult and are even seriously threatened.

I. Freedom of speech had emerged in the fifteenth and sixteenth centuries as one of the manifestations of freedom of conscience and belief. But it had acquired quickly enough its own character in becoming the liberty to form and to express an opinion. The French Declaration of the Rights of Man said, "No-one may be ('inquiété') oppressed on account of his opinions." But the Universal Declaration (Article 19) says, "Everyone has the right to freedom of opinion and expression. This right includes freedom to hold opinions without interference and to seek, receive and impart information and ideas through any media and regardless of frontiers."

It may be said that this is one of the most fundamental freedoms of man, for no-one has the power to control his internal thoughts and feelings, nor to prevent him from outwardly expressing his thoughts and feelings. Moreover, the freedom of objection and of discussion is one of the surest sources of truth.

(A) This freedom is one that appears in many forms from many sources.

Originally it was the spoken word, the prime form of expression which was used most often: the profession of faith, political opinions, public speeches and discussions (as at Hyde Park) or among friends.

But freedom of speech is used in the Church, in the family, at work (parliaments, clubs), in the universities (havens of liberty) and in schools. The study of the independence of teaching and academic freedom is very instructive: it is affirmed by the Universal Declaration and certain declarations appearing in the documents of UNESCO.

In the second place, freedom of expression manifests itself in writing (letters, pamphlets, tracts, gazettes, manuscripts), dramatic presentations (the theatre).

It has, since Gutenberg, manifested itself in print (light or heavy, journal or book). The regime of the Press has only become organised slowly in different countries; but in democratic countries it to a large extent enjoys freedom from censorship.

This freedom of expression of the journalist is linked with the right of the reader to be informed. Respect for this freedom is the test of a democratic regime.

In recent times, as a result of scientific discoveries, we have seen considerable growth in the means of communication of thoughts and opinions: the telegraph, the telephone, the gramophone or gramophone record, the radio, the telex, the use of Telstar, are examples.

The radio, the cinema, television provide facilities for communication with such large numbers of people that they are called mass media.

As regards writing and printing, their diffusion has been increased considerably by rapid printing machines, by the mechanical reproduction of writings and newspapers: copying by photographic and electronic means. A newspaper recently announced that in Japan they are about to develop the electronic reproduction of a televised newspaper as an ordinary newspaper. Let us not forget the tape-recorder, which is very convenient, but may be used without the knowledge of the speaker and be turned to the ends of somebody wishing to interfere in his private life.

(B) I have sufficiently described the changes mentioned above to speak of their influence on the conditions of the exercise of the freedom of speech and of expression, which in appearance are so simple. It is the *industrial character* of the means for transmission of thought that dominates the modern period; for one thing, industrial methods are so costly that they are beyond the reach of individuals and even of very weak groups. Press enterprises are obliged to amalgamate in order to survive: the old, small enterprises are dead or threatened. Radio and television can only be exploited by strong groups and very often are subject to a state monopoly. In spite of the text of the European Convention of 4 November 1950 which proclaims freedom of expression and of the exploitation of these means (this is the case in Europe), the

European Commission, seized of a complaint, has declared that it is necessary to take account of the practices existing at the time when states signed the treaty.

The threat to the exercise of freedom of expression flowing from these practices can only be averted if monopoly offices are independent of governments or if the composition of the administrative body guarantees that the different trends of opinion on all subjects, notably at times of political elections, can be equitably disseminated.

Furthermore, prior censorship, discarded for the Press in free countries, has become the rule for films.

The practical defence of freedom of expression more than any other freedom cannot be left to the discretion of the administration. There is no other matter which requires to the same extent independent tribunals (judicial or administrative) capable of breaking down illegal obstacles to the exercise of the legitimate freedom of speech and of expression and of refusing to pronounce unjustifiable penal condemnations against those found guilty of words or writing against public security, the security of the State or good relations among citizens (racial provocation).

It is necessary that there should be independent judges who can evaluate properly the limits on freedoms even when there are written texts. In authoritarian countries, it is always by recourse to incriminations of this kind that authority, which has no wish to repress or prevent directly by force, acts to stifle opposition and the freedom of writers.

Even in free countries, the new modes of expression are not entirely subject to the same regime as the press. Undoubtedly, persons defamed by television may resort to judicial proceedings against those who defame them. But the right of reply, existing in many countries to answer effectively accusations and attacks in the press, is only recognised in a few countries in the case of radio and television. Moreover, laws are necessary to repress interference with private life that may be made by the surveillance of words spoken by individuals; for example, telephone-tapping and the abuse of minute and secret tape recorders. The computer, which is being used more and more widely at the present time, constitutes an even more important means of information storage and communication, but also contains a potential threat to the privacy of the individual.

II. It would appear that the right of assembly has escaped changes as serious and important as those undergone by the freedom of expression. That is not so at all.

(A) The Universal Declaration declares in Article 20, "Everyone has the right to freedom of peaceful assembly and association".

It thus affirms the right of assembly as one of the manifestations of freedom of expression of a collective character, but which is distinct from freedom of association by virtue of its *temporary* nature. Assembly has been defined as "constituting a temporary group of persons formed with a view to hearing an exposition of ideas or of opinions, or with a view to joining together for the defence of interests". Its provisional character is complemented by the idea of organisation and by the object of the meeting.

For a long time, assembly was one of those acts which had to be authorised by those in power. Then a liberal phase ensued. In France, it was the law of 30 June 1881 which proclaimed the right of free assembly and the law of 28 March 1907 relieved promoters of assemblies from any obligation to give notice. But the latter obligation was re-established by the ordinance of Algiers of 30 November 1943, which was introduced into Metropolitan France on 9 August 1944.

Assembly has always been the subject of regulation. For one thing, the police authority may prohibit a meeting if it fears that it "may be of such a nature that the peace may be disturbed".

The prefects may even forbid any meeting in a given place; even private meetings can be the subject of analagous prohibitions.

(B) In reality, the growing trend towards intolerance constitutes a serious threat to freedom.

In fact, when a meeting is announced, other groups often mobilise and issue a parallel announcement in such a way that the *threat of trouble induces the authorities to prohibit the first meeting*: so much so that the intervention of the police must often play a part if freedom of assembly is to be assured.

In France, the Council of State (Conseil d'Etat) has often heard appeals on this subject; basically, it is the Courts which guarantee both the freedom and the right of supervision of the Mayor and the Prefect.

In England I believe that the position is equally delicate. The Riot Act of 1769 confers on the public authorities extensive powers in relation to the obstruction of the public highway as well as against the threat of a disturbance of the peace.

The right of assembly is distinct from demonstrations and gatherings using the *highway*. Processions, assemblies and, generally, demonstrations on the highway must in principle be the subject of prior notice if they are organised in advance (this allows them to be protected or forbidden). But very often *gatherings* form without having been announced in advance. It is these which give the public authorities the greatest anxiety. They are subjected to a repressive regime.

The evolution which I indicated at the beginning of this lecture has taken place as much in the sphere of the right of assembly as in other fields. It is no secret that in many countries the whole community is shaken by permanent assemblies and violent demonstrations of young people who call themselves hippies, or maoists, or leftists. Some of them resort to violence and depredations which do not appear to be sufficiently prevented, suppressed or redressed by the rules of the ordinary law. As a result special laws are passed. In France the "loi anti-casseurs" of 8 June 1970 has this object in mind.

In fact, this reaction by a frightened society could have been very dangerous for the liberties of all citizens, especially trade union processions. Fortunately, the law which the Parliament of France passed was comparatively moderate.

But this latest episode confirms that public liberties are always precarious, always threatened. In our changing society, human rights must be constantly protected by the Judge, whether in support of the administration when that body is defending liberties or against private people and against the public powers, when it is they who threaten or suffocate freedom.

This protection accorded by an independent judge is so precious that, on the international plane, there is a growing movement to entrust the supervision of states' behaviour to commissions composed of competent and impartial persons whose duty it is to establish the facts, prepare recommendations and, sometimes, to obtain certain reparations from governments found guilty of violations.

In the ultimate analysis, it is to the international judge that one must confide the task of deciding whether a human right has or has not been violated. But we should not deceive ourselves into thinking that it will not be a long time before law will triumph in relations between states. Meanwhile a tenacious and ceaseless struggle must be steadfastly carried on, notably by the education of the younger generation, for there can be no peace if human rights are not respected.

4. Race, Poverty and Population
(An Internationalist's view)

© LORD CARADON

[Lord Caradon explained,* by way of introduction, that, although he was by experience an administrator, he was by strong inclination a politician. However, on that occasion he was speaking not as a politician but as an impatient internationalist: and, not so much about present conflicts and confrontations as about the future, about the greater dominating dangers of race and poverty and population. He drew attention to the fallacy of the alleged conflict between British interests and international interests.

"The fact is," said Lord Caradon, "that no country in the world needs international peace more than ours. No country in the world needs a prosperous, thriving, developing third world more than ours. No country could give a better lead than ours in fighting the three monsters – the evil of racialism, the degradation of poverty and the pollution of over-population."]

Three World Dangers in One

I have said that I chose to speak to you today not about the immediate conflicts and confrontations. I do not propose to speak this evening about the arrival of the People's Republic of China in the United Nations, nor about the need to bring the peoples of the Middle East to a Peace Conference, nor even about the necessity for mounting economic and political pressure to make the white regimes of southern Africa bring the Africans into consultation and partnership.

I have selected the much more difficult subjects of race and poverty and population. We could settle all the disputes and conflicts. China could become the most reasonable and constructive member of the United Nations. Permanent peace could be achieved in the Middle East on the basis of the unanimous Security Council resolution. The racial regimes of southern Africa could

* The Editor accepts full responsibility for this summary of Lord Caradon's introductory remarks.

be reformed or replaced. All that could be achieved, and still the world could be hurtling headlong like the Gaderene swine to disaster.

We must keep the peace. But it is at least equally important to try to make the peace tolerable. Better perhaps to be obliterated by the bomb than for countless millions to sink and die in helpless and hopeless squalor.

So let us look beyond the broken ground of current disputes, and beyond the foothills of existing conflicts. They must certainly be crossed. Today let us look to the greater mountain peaks beyond, the peaks which must be surmounted if mankind is to survive.

What is the most important thing to understand about race, poverty and population? I think that the most important thing of all to be realised is that they are not three separate dangers. They are all one. It is to that main theme, the three world dangers in one, that I want to speak today.

If we could separate out the three problems, deal with each of the three at leisure, isolate each, that would be a comfort and an insurance. But we cannot.

The millions who are sucked into the urban slums of Asia and Africa are not white people. The millions who hopelessly seek employment in the so-called developing countries are not Europeans. The millions of women who are condemned in their teens to a life-time slavery of non-stop child bearing are not members of the Women's Liberation Movement.

The Western world invented pollution, unemployment, industrial squalor, but the white minority is becoming intent on escaping from them and has the means to do so. If money can win, New York will survive, but in Calcutta there is precious little money and practically no hope. The sentence there is more than a life sentence. There is no hope of choice for parents or children, for this generation or the next. There is no expectation of escape.

The white people, the minority of mankind, retreat from the towns and from reality to their segregated suburbs, they grow steadily more remote and more affluent and more replete to the point of obese saturation. They are the well-favoured and fat-fleshed kine of the parable in the Bible, who were eaten up, you will remember, by the ill-favoured and lean-fleshed kine who followed them. The well-favoured few in the old countries will surely be in danger, as the parable told us, from the lean-fleshed many in the rest of the world.

The three interlocked monster dangers of race and poverty and population threaten not only to degrade but also to divide the world and if we fail in dealing with one of the dangers we shall fail in dealing with them all.

It was Sir Alec Douglas Home who said when he was Prime Minister: "I believe the greatest danger ahead of us is that the world might be divided on racial lines. I see no danger, not even the nuclear bomb, which could be so catastrophic as that." Yes, that is the catastrophe which comes nearer. And the dangers of race are complicated beyond calculation by the addition of the dangers of poverty and population. Together the three dangers far exceed the old dangers of division by religion and division by ideology.

Division and degradation go together. The danger so often stated but so seldom grasped is the danger of the gulf growing ever wider and ever more rapidly between the minority, the comfortable, complacent, affluent, white people of the older nations on the one hand and, on the other, the majority, overcrowded, impoverished, discontented, the coloured people of the new nations – the great majority of mankind.

We could easily spend all our time today gaping at advancing horrors.

Look at the confrontation on the River Zambesi in Africa with African nationalism on one side and white supremacy on the other. Who can believe or who can be confident that the confrontation will be peacefully resolved? And if race conflict flares up in Africa then all Africa will be inflamed and surely the whole world involved.

Look at the figures on poverty, with a rough comparison between an average annual income of less than a hundred pounds per head a year in the poor countries and an average of more than a thousand pounds per head per year in the richer countries. And the economists tell us that while with luck the average amongst the poor nations might possibly in this development decade advance by a half from a hundred to a hundred and fifty pounds, the average in the rich countries, so they also tell us, may well in the same period double from one to nearer two thousand. And

you hear people still talking glibly about narrowing the gap between rich and poor. Nonsense; the gap is growing all the time
rapidly greater. The poor nations are being left far behind.

What is more, before long more than half of the world will live
in tropical urban slums, and maybe half of those who inhabit these
stagnant swamps of human degradation will be unemployed.
That's where most of the children of the new generation will be
brought up, in conditions unfit for animals.

And all the time the tide of population comes flowing in –
another million every week.

I shall not weary you with statistics. We are all too familiar
with the seemingly fantastic figures. It does us no harm perhaps
for our noses to be rubbed in the terrifying facts. But I am
anxious to expiate no more about the dangers. Surely we can all
see them now. I am more anxious to speak about action.

The worst thing that could happen would be that we should
despair, that the dangers would seem staggering, overwhelming,
that we should give up and turn away, that we should fail to search
for effective action, that we should bury our heads in suburban
selfishness, that we should disregard the call to stand between the
living and the dead and stay the plague.

Action On Race

First of all, the best thing we could do would be to expose, to
discredit, to eliminate the hypocrites. The worst offenders are
those who denounce apartheid and racial discrimination with a
pharisee's pomposity, and at the same time by their actions sustain
and delight those who preach and practise racial domination and
injustice. Sell arms to the South African Government, they say,
oppose United Nations in South West Africa, pat the Portuguese
on the back, trust the illegal regime in Rhodesia, defy both the
Commonwealth and the United Nations, put this country on the
wrong side in the great racial issues of the world – but at the same
time never fail to speak ill of the system which your actions so
greatly encourage and support. That is the hypocrisy which is so
nauseating.

Increasingly it is realised that there are three possible policies
for southern Africa – one is appeasement, another is violence, and
the third is unremitting, persistent, mounting pressure, pressure
by the international community, pressure to insist and require

that the oppression and the subjection of the African majorities must give way to participation and co-operation.

Yes, and dialogue too. I am all in favour of dialogue. But the dialogue should not only be with selected and conducted visitors, the dialogue should first be with the African majorities of southern Africa and their chosen leaders. The African majorities are silent majorities, silent because they are not expected or permitted to speak, silent because on the issues vital to them – issues of their lives and liberties – no one consults them, no one speaks to them. They are not only bound but also gagged. They cannot afford to be deaf to the orders of their white masters, but they are required and condemned to be dumb. South African Dialogue so far has been for export only. If internal dialogue is still opposed, then it should be imported.

Appeasement from outside southern Africa might put off the racial explosion but in the end it would greatly increase its devastating force. As Winston Churchill used to say "Things do not get better by being left alone. Unless they are adjusted they explode with a shattering detonation". Appeasement from outside encourages the oppressors, and discourages the oppressed. It puts off the evil day, but it makes sure that when it comes the day will be far more evil.

Violence is no answer either. It may one day be inevitable, but it is the last answer. To rely on violence would be to despair, and to accept the necessity of even greater human suffering on a scale not yet imagined.

The white supremacy regimes of southern Africa will not be won over by kind words. No will they be quickly overcome by guerilla terror. The only hope of avoiding even more terrible consequences of hate and blood is to maintain and step up the pressure. The necessary fundamental change in southern African policies will be achieved in no other way.

Action on Poverty
Just as international action is the only answer in the issues of race, so must international action also provide the strength of the campaign against poverty. Fortunately the past few decades have shown the way. Even as recently as twenty years ago the idea of the campaign against poverty being an international responsibility had scarcely emerged. It is still in its infancy. But the United

Nations Development Programme now provides a proved instrument for economic development. Still wholly inadequate in financial resources and at present in the throes of reorganisation, but already proved in method and effectiveness.

Statistics cannot convey the range and the variety of the early achievements of the United Nations Development Programme (UNDP), with over fifteen hundred major pre-investment projects which have already stimulated over five thousand million dollars of follow-up financing. In addition there have been more than five hundred large-scale education and training projects and well over three hundred applied research projects and fifty major projects in development planning, and many thousand smaller scale technical assistance missions.

Not a bad start, in little more than a decade. All this is practical pioneering – discovering new resources, harnessing neglected power, attacking disease and waste and pollution, new crops, new skills, new methods, all opening up new opportunities.

Moreover the Programme is sustained by growing voluntary contributions from over a hundred nations and, perhaps the most striking feature of all, the receiving poorer nations contribute more to UNDP development projects than the rich donor countries.

This is the new living thing in the world. A wide acceptance of international responsibility for a universal attack on the degradation of poverty everywhere in the world – that is the idea whose time has come.

Development aid is no longer merely a mixture of charitable condescension and political favourtism by a few rich nations. It is now increasingly recognised as an international co-operative multilateral enterprise in the equal interest of poor and rich alike in a world which could be united.

Action on Population
It was in the realm of population that the world woke up last to the necessity of international action. If the idea of multilateral development aid was born in the fifties, the idea of international action to stem the population flood did not emerge till the late sixties. The idea has very rapidly taken hold in the past five or six years. Looking back it seems incredible that ten years ago the idea of international action in population control was almost unheard of.

If I had to point to a date when the world woke up to that idea I would recall Human Rights Day in 1966 when the twelve States made their famous Declaration. Be it noted that they were not the rich white nations who made the appeal. They were the so-called developing nations whose future prospects, whose stability, whose very existence depends on saving themselves from drowning in the population flood. They called, you remember, on leaders around the world to join with them in "this great challenge for the well-being and happiness of people everywhere".

Let me restate my own personal convictions about population control in five positive propositions:

(i) For the individual. It is a matter of freedom, a matter of setting the individual free, free from the prison of poverty and ignorance and prejudice, free to choose. Without the right and the means to choose there is no freedom.

(ii) For the family. The purpose should surely be to make the family not a burden but a blessing. The family deserves better than to be the outcome of ignorance. The family is too important to be merely a creature of chance.

(iii) For the child. We must put first – first of all – the aim, the overriding aim, to give every child born into the world some reasonable expectation of survival and some hope of living in human dignity.

(iv) For the nation. I quote again the famous declaration made by the twelve Heads of State on Human Rights Day in 1966 – "We believe that the population problem must be recognised as a principal element in long-range national planning if governments are to achieve their economic goals and fulfill the aspirations of their people".

(v) For the international community. The President of the World Bank, Robert McNamara, constantly reminds us that "the greatest single obstacle to the economic and social advancement of the majority of the peoples of the under-developed world is rampant population growth . . . We can meet this challenge if we have the wisdom and the moral energy to do so. But if we lack these qualities, then I fear we lack the means of survival on this planet."

I say that if we bring children into the world without giving them some reasonable expectation of survival and some hope of human dignity, it will be a waste, a criminal waste, an utterly unforgiveable waste, of the most precious thing in the world, the potentiality of the human personality.

Now, I am glad to say, the international community hastens to make up for the lost time. The General Assembly of the United Nations, the United Nations Development Programme, the World Bank, the UN Specialised Agencies, all co-operate in the campaign. Now the whole cavalcade is on the move. The United Nations Population Fund made up of voluntary contributions is already measured in terms of tens of millions of dollars annually. Advice and assistance go out from UN Headquarters to any and every country which seeks such aid.

Effective International Action

Again the action is essentially international. The dangers of the world are far too great to be dealt with by one nation or one group of nations however rich or powerful. Whether it is in race or poverty or population it is international action which is vital – international action which must be decisive.

No one maintains that what has been started is more than a beginning. But the instrument is there – sharp, effective, available. I constantly repeat that there is nothing wrong with the United Nations except the Members. The instrument is fine. All we have to do to make use of it is to agree. The Russians are blunt. They say that we were lucky to get agreement on the United Nations Charter in 1945. We probably wouldn't get it if we had to negotiate for it now. Make the best of it, they say. I agree with them.

I have little patience with those who talk of drastic revision of the Charter. It isn't going to happen. We don't need a better Charter: what we do desperately need is a stronger will to use it.

What a remarkable advance has indeed been made since 1945 without any substantial revision of the Charter. The United Nations has shown that it can adapt its Charter to new needs. In 1945 it was barely imagined that most of the work of the United Nations would be in the economic and social fields as it is today. International effort to prevent race war, to tackle poverty, to control population are new ideas. They have emerged since 1945. This year, 1971, has been declared by the General Assembly as the international year against racial discrimination; next year is the year of the International Conference on Environment in Stockholm; 1974 has already been declared as World Population Year.

These are the new frontier preoccupations of the international community. In all these issues the initiative has been taken within the United Nations. So it is that the instrument of the United Nations has shown itself not only effective but also adaptable, the new enterprise of the United Nations is not following but leading, not behind the times but ahead.

The Obligation of Optimism

I must try to get the balance right. Do not, I beg you, imagine that I live in a world of imaginative euphoria, that I have no knowledge of the hard facts and harsh truths of international life. On the contrary I have often seen at first hand in different parts of the world the cruelty and the futility of violence. I have suffered, as few can have suffered, the weariness, the exhaustion, of listening to interminable speeches and reading piles of deadly dull documents, all day long and often far into the night. I am a leading expert in international frustration. Often in the General Assembly I remembered Wordsworth's lines:

> Earth is sick
> And Heaven is weary
> Of the hollow words
> Which States and Kingdoms utter
> When they speak of Truth and Justice.

But while I have no illusions I am not disillusioned. I wish to persuade you that while the forces of conflict and hate and greed and fear are strong and well organised and often well led, the powers of conciliation and compassion are potentially victorious.

Even more I should like to persuade you that if we exert ourselves, if we shake off inertia, and if we despise complacency, if we are ready to make a great effort of understanding and of initiative and of persistence, the barriers can be overcome. I have not many heroes, but one man above others I love and admire. I refer to Ralph Bunche with whom I had the honour to work for many years at the United Nations, and who now lies gravely ill. Listen to the simple words he used when he was speaking not long ago to his own University of California.

This is what he said:

For more than a quarter of a century now I have been engaged in work in which hopefulness is an imperative qualification; one must believe that man can be saved – or salvaged – from his inevitable frailties and follies, that all problems of human relations are soluble, that conflict situations, even those in the Middle East and on university campuses, however deep-seated and prolonged, can be resolved, that a world at peace is in fact attainable. Otherwise one's work, all diplomacy, the United Nations itself, become a fateful travesty and all mankind would be utterly doomed.

I like to remember too what was said of another reformer in the last century. "The devil with sad and sober sense on his grey face tells the rulers of the world that the misery that disfigures the life of great societies is beyond reach of human remedy. A voice is raised from time to time in answer; a challenge in the name of the mercy of God, or the justice of nature or the dignity of man." Such a voice is that of Ralph Bunche.

It is men like Ralph Bunche who answer the call and the cause of international action. If there is one thing I have learnt in the ten years of experience of the new parliamentary diplomacy at the United Nations it is that international action needs individual initiative. Time and again I have seen an international situation changed by the initiative of one country or one man.

When Ambassador Pardo of Malta insisted on his resolution to make the riches of the deep sea bed the heritage of all mankind. When Deputy Foreign Minister Kutznetzov referred back to his government at the last moment to get their agreement to abandon the Soviet resolution on the Middle East and vote for ours. When Ambassador Pierson Dixon of the United Kingdom scorned a victory to work for a success on Cyprus. When Foreign Minister Paul Henri Spaak of Belgium won over the Security Council by his eloquence even when speaking of the Congo. When Ralph Bunche flew through the night to Geneva to save the negotiations on Bahrain. Time after time I have seen men with the new motive of international understanding and agreement break away from a deadlock, cut through the confusion, shame the cowards and astonish the time-servers.

It is certainly true that the dangers I speak of – of race and poverty and population combined – are greater than the world has ever known before. But it is my conviction that the new generation will respond to these greater challenges, will detest discrimination and resist oppression and resent poverty and hate pollution and despise defeatism. I believe that the new generation will rejoice that it has such ugly evils to fight, and will say with St Paul – if I may repeat my favourite text for international affairs:

And not only so, but we glory in tribulations also, knowing that tribulations worketh patience and patience experience and experience hope.

Personal Convictions

Now before I finish I beg you to forgive me if I try to formulate the convictions which have taken shape in my mind from my own experience of international tribulations. Not so long ago I saw it reported in one of our Sunday newspapers that Tory leaders specially disliked something they called "Caradonism". I need not tell you that I was greatly flattered and elated to have achieved such a distinction. I conjured up illusions of self-importance; I began to think of the cult of Caradonism gaining ground and even becoming fashionable in world affairs.

I hope you will not think me unduly vain if I tell you what Caradonism is. Some, from the sound radical left, may think that my stated convictions are obvious platitudes. Some, from the reactionary right, may say that my ideas are wild, dangerous, revolutionary. The people I most dislike are those who pay lip service to these purposes but are secretly resolved to frustrate them. My hope and belief is that amongst the new generation there is already an eagerness to agree and to accept, a determination to work, and a readiness to fight, if necessary, for these aims.

Here is how I would sum up the propositions I commend to you:

(i) We must recognise that the problems of race and poverty and population which threaten to degrade and divide the world are in effect all one; they cry out for international action.

(ii) We must mobilise international opinion, particularly in the new generation, to deal with these dangers.

(iii) We should first resolve never to accept or tolerate or encourage or support the evils of racial domination and racial discrimination and racial injustice.

(iv) We should further be determined to use every method of persuasion and pressure to being home to those who perpetuate racial injustice that their policies will never be internationally accepted or condoned, but will lead them only to international contempt and isolation and, if persisted in, sooner or later to disaster.

(v) We must strengthen and accelerate the international effort to achieve rapid economic development in the third world to save the majority of mankind from deeper descent into the pit of greater poverty and illiteracy and unemployment and squalor.

(vi) We must realise that economic development in the poorer countries without limitation of population will utterly fail; both human compassion and economic necessity demand international action to supplement voluntary and national endeavour in population control.

(vii) We should hope and trust and require that in all these purposes Great Britian will now go forward and put her international experience and her world-wide interests to the best use by taking an honourable lead.

(viii) We must believe that even the great and growing dangers of the world are not beyond the reach of human remedy; we must be content with no narrow or exclusive or defeatist nationalism; our campaign and our concern and our compassion and our ambition should be for men and women everywhere.

So much for Caradonism. I would be sad to think that such aims are to be denigrated or despised or discarded. I see no reason why our role in the world need miserably shrink. It was Edmund Burke, you remember, who said that a great empire and little minds go ill together. God forbid that having ended the great empire we should be stuck with the little minds.

My belief is that, being rid of an empire and no longer a superpower we are free and able to exercise a greater and more beneficent leadership in the international world than ever before.

And what is more, I believe that the new generation in this country is not prepared to see such urgent and exciting opportunities rejected. The old men may become isolationist, the young ones will insist on being international.

I confidently believe that on these world issues the new generation will put the older generation to shame.

It is those of the younger generation who say in famous words:

But you have the power, you have the wealth, you have rank, you have organisation, you have the place of power. What have we? We think we have the people's heart. We believe and we know that we have the harvest of the future.

5. *Freedom of Association and the Right to Work*

© LORD DENNING

In England, Human Rights are not guaranteed by any written constitution, as they are in other countries. They are guaranteed by the decisions of the judges. If you look into the United Nations Charter, or if you look into the great written constitutions of the world, you will find the principles set down in legislative form; but not so in England. You have to look for them in the precedents which have been laid down by the judges. Perhaps I may remind you of the question which Tennyson was asked: "You ask me why I stay in England?" His answer was: "It is the land where – A man may speak the thing he will. A land of settled government. A land of just and old renown where Freedom slowly broadens down from precedent to precedent." We, in the courts over the centuries, have sought to guarantee the freedom of the individual – his freedom to think what he will, to say what he will, to go where he will, on all his lawful occasions, without hindrance from anyone save as permitted by law.

But in these days we must not look solely to the freedom of the individual. We must look to the security of the individual. This depends on the maintenance of law and order. What good is a man's freedom to him, if his home is liable to be ransacked by burglars and thieves, or his womenfolk assaulted, or if hooligans break up the trains on which he travels, or if mobs invade a private dinner party and break it up by violence? When such things happen, can a man think what he will? Can he say what he will? Can he go where he will? The essential guarantee of freedom is the maintenance of law and order. Many of the rights which are under discussion today are not to be found in any of the written constitutions. I refer to the right to dissent, the right to demonstrate, the right to strike, the right to work. Let me go through them: firstly, the right to dissent. It is part and parcel of our freedom of speech which was established in this country by the verdicts of juries. The great case was two hundred years ago. A letter-writer called Junius – we don't know his identity, it was a *nom de plume* – wrote in the *London Evening Post* that the King (who was the executive government of the day) did not know the language of truth till he heard it in the complaints of his subjects. The printers and publishers were charged before Lord Mansfield with seditious libel. For once that great judge had got his law wrong. He said the question of libel or no libel was for the judge, not the jury: and that all that the jury had to say was whether the words were printed and published or not – which they clearly were. It was, in effect, a direction to the jury to find the printers and publishers Guilty. The jury went out. They went out for five and a half hours, so long that Lord Mansfield went back to his home in Bloomsbury Square awaiting the verdict. Then they came back. In defiance of that great judge they found the printers and publishers Not Guilty. It is said that the hurrahs and huzzahs reverberated across the metropolis until they reached the ears of Lord Mansfield himself in Bloomsbury Square. That verdict established the freedom of the press – the freedom of speech – in England to criticise the government of the day.

Just one further instance from that period of history. It arose when Tom Paine, the pamphleteer, wrote a pamphlet on the Rights of Man. He had the audacity to suggest that the constitution of England should be changed so as to be like that of France. He was charged with seditious libel. He instructed an advocate to defend him – Thomas Erskine, the greatest advocate of the time. Great pressure was brought on Erskine to return the brief. Lord Lough-borough met him as he was going over Hampstead Heath and said, "Erskine, you must return Paine's brief." "But", Erskine replied, "I have accepted it, and I must do it". When he came to address the jury, he used these memorable words: "I will forever, and at all hazards, uphold the dignity, independence and integrity of the English Bar, without which impartial justice, the most valued part of the English Constitution, can have no place."

Then, remembering that the advocates have a monopoly of audience in the courts, he went on: "For the moment that any advocate can be permitted to say that he will, or will not, stand between the Crown and the subject, in the courts in which he daily sits to practice, from that day the liberties of England are at an end."

There you have two great instances of the right to dissent, the right to criticise the government of the day, the right to advocate even a change in constitutions established by the law. That is one of the fundamental human rights.

Next, the right to demonstrate. It is only part and parcel of the right of free speech, the right to advocate the cause in which you believe. Dissent is by voice. Demonstration is by marches and placards. I can give a modern illustration. It is the great new motorway in West London, which is to be thronged with noisy, smelly vehicles. When the Parliamentary Secretary came to cut the tape, a crowd of demonstrators waved banners reading "Motorway Pollution?" "Stop the Noise." A great placard said, "Get us out of this hell. Rehouse us now." It was a lawful demonstration. It had its effect. The GLC agreed to rehouse them.

The right to demonstrate is part of our right to free speech. It must always be upheld as such. But – and there is a "but" – it must be by lawful means and not by unlawful. A good end never justifies a bad means. The sooner that is known the better. Take a recent case when Mr Enoch Powell went to address an audience of students. He was to address them as I address you now. A small minority group at the back shouts him down. That was unlawful. Those students had not learned the very first lesson of democracy – that freedom of speech means freedom of speech, not only for the views of which you approve, but also for the views which you wholeheartedly detest. Take another demonstration. A group of forty or fifty students at the University of Aberystwyth chartered a coach. They came up to the Law Courts in the Strand. Mr Justice Lawton was trying an important case with which they had nothing whatever to do. They filled the public gallery. They strolled into the well of the court. They shouted slogans. They sang songs in Welsh. They broke up the hearing. But to their credit, it must be said, they did not use violence. The Judge dealt with them. Some apologised. They were fined £50. Fourteen did not apologise. They were sentenced immediately for contempt of court to three months imprisonment. Eleven appealed to the Court of Appeal. Although they did not apologise, they submitted to the jurisdiction of the court. Thus they recognised the rule of the law. They had a good legal argument, namely, that on the wording of the statute the sentences ought to have been suspended. But that argument did not prevail. A judge has power to imprison straightaway for contempt of court. The sentence need not be suspended. Those students had not learned the elementary lesson that, if you strike at the cause of justice in this land, you strike at the basis of society on which all freedoms depend. So they had to be taught a lesson. I may add, however, that we took into account the goodness of the cause in which they believed – that the Welsh language should be equal in Wales with English. So we reduced the three months to seven days. They were freed at once. There was an interesting reaction. From England I had letters or postcards – all anonymous – accusing the court. One postcard said "You lousy coward". Another said "You ought to resign". But from Wales it was very different. From the heads of colleges and universities, from distinguished preachers, I had letters, signed letters, saying that the decision had a most steadying influence in Wales and it had done good for the rule of law.

I have one more instance of demonstration. It is a very different one. In Cambridge, a group of people were sitting down in a restaurant having a meal. It was to support visits to Greece. It so happened that Greece was then under a regime of which some members of their university greatly disapproved. They were entitled to demonstrate against the regime. But what did they do? Instead of using lawful means, they used violence. They destroyed the freedom of others. They went further. They even assaulted the police – the police who are the first line of defence in a civilised society. The Judge passed severe sentences. They were upheld by the Court of Appeal. It effectively stopped such violence by students. In a civilised society we must maintain, not only the right to demonstrate, but also the right of all to say and think what they will. No-one by "sitting-in" or the like is entitled to force his own views, on those of the majority. No-one is entitled to take the law into his own hands.

A word now about the right of association – the right to meet together to advance your aims. We did not attain it in England until the last 100 years. In 1819 a great crowd of people came together in fields outside Manchester, Peterfield. There were 60,000 of them. They waved banners calling for "Universal Suffrage". They wished to abolish the "rotten boroughs" where the squires could put their nominees into Parliament. The magistrates were terrified at the size of this meeting. They called out the yeomanry who charged them with cutlasses. They killed a dozen and injured hundreds. The "ringleaders" were charged before the judges. They were sentenced to imprisonment and to transportation for having taken part in that demonstration. To its credit, the Common Council of the City of London protested. They proclaimed "the right of all citizens to meet together in lawful assembly to deliberate on public grievances". A few years later the farm labourers of Hampshire, my own county, gathered together. They were only getting half-a-crown a week. They wanted, I think, an additional sixpence. Their meetings were perfectly orderly. But they were said to be guilty of unlawful assembly. They were sentenced to transportation. Until 1871 it was unlawful for workers to combine together to try and raise their wages, or to get better conditions. It was an illegal and criminal conspiracy. Now, by statute, that has all been altered.

We have the freedom of association of any group to meet to forward its cause so long as it does so by lawful means. But in 1906 trade unions were put in one respect above the law. They were exempt from any action for doing wrong. Gradually, however, the Courts have been bringing them back within the law. There was in 1954 the case of Mr Bonsor. He was a member of the Musicians Union. It was a closed shop. He fell into arrears with his subscriptions for a week or two. On that event the secretary said that he was no longer a member of that union. As a result, he could not get work anywhere. Nowhere could he play his music. He was reduced to scraping the rust off Brighton Pier. He brought an action against the trade union. The trade union said, "We are exempt from any action of law." It was held, however, that the secretary had acted unlawfully in expelling Mr Bonsor. The House of Lords held that a trade union could be sued for the wrong done to him. But, unfortunately, the case had lasted so long Mr Bonsor had died before a decision was given in his favour.

We had another case last summer. Mr Edwards was a member of a union, one of the printing trade unions. He happened to be a coloured man. An arrangement was made whereby his contributions to the union would not be paid by him direct. They would be paid by his employers on his behalf to the union. By the mistake of the union secretary it was not done. So technically Mr Edwards had not paid his subscriptions to the union. For that, according to the rules, he was automatically expelled from the union. There was an automatic forfeiture clause. There were four others, white people, in the same position. They were allowed to pay up those subscriptions. Not so Mr Edwards. The union would not accept any payment up by him; so he remained expelled. Later they admitted that his expulsion was unlawful and had to pay damages. The Court said that the "automatic forfeiture" clause was invalid. It could be an instrument of oppression. If a man, by oversight, fell into arrears with one or two subscriptions, others could force him out of the industry.

So we have gradually established the right to work. It has been a long haul. It was derived from the "club" cases of the last century, when it was held that the committee could not turn a man out of a club without hearing him. From it we have gradually evolved the right of every man to work.

In the cases I have quoted up till now, the man was already a member of the union. It is much more difficult when he is not yet a member, but wants to join. It is like a man who wants to join an Inn of Court or a university. Is there uncontrolled discretion in the professional bodies to refuse? A hundred and forty years ago, a young man wanted to join Lincoln's Inn. The judges said the benchers had an uncontrolled discretion. They could be as arbitrary and capricious as they chose. They could refuse to admit him. The same would seem to apply to a university, and to a trade union. But the judges have gradually altered that law. We had a case where a lady, Mrs Nagle, trained horses for the race course. The Jockey Club have a virtual monopoly over race courses. They can license horse racing. They can license the people to be trainers. Mrs Nagle was a woman. The Jockey Club said, "We never license a woman to be a trainer". For twenty years Mrs Nagle was not licensed herself but her lad was. Then she brought an action before the courts to test the position. It was held that when a body has a monopoly of an important activity, they cannot act arbitrarily or capriciously. The Jockey Club gave way. Now Mrs Nagle is licensed with the Jockey Club.

We cannot always manage it. There was a Mr Faramus who was a member of the Musicians Union. He had been a member for eight or nine years. Some members of the Council took objection to him. They did not want him to be a member any more. They looked up the records. They found that twenty or thirty years ago, in Jersey during the German occupation, he had been guilty of some minor offence. It was something trifling. The rules said,

"No one who has been guilty of a criminal offence is admissible to be a member". They invoked that rule and said that Mr Faramus was never a member of this union, and that he had never been a member, although he had belonged for eight or nine years and paid all his subscriptions. The House of Lords upheld that decision.

Let me add one word about the right to demonstrate. Although I have said that unlawful means must not be used, nevertheless I must add this point: there is a duty on those in authority to pay regard to what is said by those who dissent and those who demonstrate. If a complaint is justified, they should give effect to it. If it is unjustified, they should give their reasons. Their duty to listen is co-relative to the duty to use lawful means. So it is not all one-sided. In many cases, the reason for the demonstration is because people feel they cannot get justice in any other way. They feel strongly that their voice will not be heard, so they resort to unlawful means, to sit-ins or even to violence. If unlawful means are to be avoided, then their grievances should be heard, and if justified they should be remedied. If there are injustices in the law, the law must be reformed. Law reform is in the air. It has been in previous centuries. One hundred and forty years ago, Lord Brougham made a great speech on law reform. It took six hours. In the House he refreshed himself from a basket of oranges which Bellamy, the butler, provided. At the end, he finished with these words:

> It was said of Augustus that he found Rome of brick and left it marble.
>
> But how much more shall be our sovereign's boast when he shall have it to say
>
> That he found law dear and left it cheap;
>
> Found it a sealed book, left it a living letter;
>
> Found it the patrimony of the rich, left it the inheritance of the poor;
>
> Found it the two-edged sword of craft and oppression, left it the staff of honesty and the shield of innocence.
>
> So we must each in our part do what we can in the aid of law reform.

When I look upon the turbulence of today, when we remember that England has been the source of law and order for many centuries, I recall Kipling's words about the meadow which is

called Runnymede between Windsor and Staines where the g...
Charter was sealed by King John over 750 years ago:

> Whenever mob or monarch lays
> Too rude a hand on English ways,
> A whisper wakes, the shadow plays
> Across the reeds at Runnymede.

To this audience I may perhaps finish with Wordsworth's words:

> We must be free or die, who speake the tongue
> That Shakespeare spake; the faith and morals hold
> Which Milton held. In every thing we are sprung
> Of Earth's first blood, have titles manifold.

ght to Live and be Free

SOR J. E. S. FAWCETT

I tн.. best to speak about the rights of men to live and to be free in the context of the European Convention on Human Rights, if only because the issues are so vast seen on a world level as to become unmanageable. But I shall of course want to say something about the United Nations Covenants. Another reason is that the issues of the "right to live and be free" which come our way and force themselves upon us are much better understood in the closer context with which we are familiar of Europe. So, if you look at the European Convention on Human Rights, you will find in Articles 2–5, giving very brief titles, the right to life, the prohibition of torture and inhuman treatment, the prohibition of slavery and servitude, and the control of detention. It is worth here making some comparison with the United Nations Civil and Political Rights Covenant, which has parallel provisions, at some points more elaborate. It seems to me that the UN Covenants are to be regarded now as the new standard of achievement even though they may not yet be in force, which replace the Universal Declaration of 1948. There are two reasons for approaching them in that way.

In the first place, they are much more extended than the Universal Declaration. If you take the right to life, the Universal Declaration has only those three words, in Article 3. But in Article 6 of the Civil and Political Rights Covenant, the right to life is considered much more carefully and particularly in the light of the whole evolution of practice on capital punishment. So, it would seem to me almost perverse to go back to the Universal Declaration if we want to know what the trend and the world view is on the right to life. For this we must look at the Covenant.

There is a second reason. The Covenant, though still not in force, was nevertheless drafted and adopted in the General Assembly by a vastly more representative number of countries than the Universal Declaration of 1948. I stress this because I think we now have too much reference back to the Universal Declaration; while I would not wish to minimise the impact of that Declaration, we have to recognise that thought and practice does evolve and change in these areas of human rights.

Another general point that comes up in the Covenants and European Convention is what is meant by fundamental rights. This really has to be understood in a minimal sense. It makes a kind of threshold which practice and administration in the various fields covered by the Convention must reach. It does not mean fundamental in an absolute sense, that there are no circumstances in which the rights and freedoms guaranteed may not be restricted or derogated from. In fact, there are few rights or freedoms in either the European Convention or the Covenants, which may not be derogated from in some circumstances.

Here, we observe a contrast between the European Convention on the one hand and the United Nations Covenants on the other. There is a certain conflict between the political concepts of the protection of rights. The Convention and the Covenant are both clearly struggling always to balance the rights and freedoms of individuals and the interests of the community. If one may speak in shorthand of a liberal conception of human rights, it tends to stress the primacy of the individual; in the last resort, it is the protection of the individual and his rights and freedoms that must prevail. This can lead in the practice of protection to some disproportion; for it seems strange to be deeply involved in finding whether an individual has suffered a minor miscarriage of justice at a time when perhaps in another context or another part of the world a great many people are under great oppression or are being wrongfully killed. But perhaps this disproportion of attention has to be. In contrast to the liberal conception, there stands the conception called Socialist in Eastern Europe, that the real source of rights and freedoms is the community, that no one has inherent rights and freedoms. The community grants or allows rights and freedoms to the individual, within the framework of the social objectives of the community and with regard to the stage that has been reached in achieving those objectives. That, of course, is a very different approach to human rights with markedly different consequences in how particular rights and freedoms are regarded.

Having made these general remarks, I would like now to come to the three of the rights which are involved in the notion of living and being free. First of all, there is the right to life itself. Here, we have an interesting example of a marked evolution in practice, so that Article 2 of the European Convention, drafted as it was in 1950, is to some extent already out of date. Capital punishment has been largely abolished in the Convention countries. It remains in one or two countries, Cyprus and Turkey for example, for crimes such as murder or treason. But broadly the change has been significant. In the Federal Republic of Germany capital punishment is totally abolished for any purpose whatsoever, and even in those countries where it is retained it is within the context of what the United Nations Civil and Political Rights Covenant calls "most serious crimes". The Inter-American Convention on Human Rights, which is dealing with countries where the practice has not evolved so far, denies the right to impose capital punishment for political offences. Here it is of some interest to note that the European Extradition Convention makes it possible for a country, which has abolished capital punishment, to refuse extradition to a country where capital punishment will or may be imposed for the extraditable offence involved. This raises an interesting point of practice in the protection of rights and the operation of the European Convention. Where you have a contrast between two countries, particularly as regards the practice of capital punishment, the question may arise whether it is right to extradite a person to the country where he may suffer capital punishment or indeed some other ill-treatment contrary to the Convention. Does the obligation of a party to the Convention extend that far, or can the government authorities say: "It is not our business or responsibility what is done in other countries." Where the other country is not a party to the Convention there is a special difficulty. This is a point which has been dealt with in the European Commission a number of times. A kind of practice has come to be established, though the Convention is not very clear about it, that where extradition or deportation is feared by an applicant to the Commission to lead to ill-treatment in some form or other, governments are prepared to hold up the procedure for expulsion till it has been possible for the Commission to look at the case more closely.

Finally, you will see in Article 6 of the Civil and Political Rights Covenant, paragraph 5, section 5, that capital punishment may not be imposed on any person below 18 years in countries where it is still applicable, and it may not be imposed on any pregnant woman.

The second rule has been the law of England, in fact, since 1931, though it raises questions of the rights of the unborn child which are now very much in dispute; and the Commission has had this issue put to it in more than one application.

Coming to the second clause of the next article, that is the prohibition of torture and inhuman treatment, we have to ask what kind of treatment this really envisages. At first glance, people might think it really obvious what is meant by torture or inhuman treatment. But when you try to apply these terms to actual situations, it becomes more difficult than perhaps appears at first sight. In the European Commission itself it has been suggested, certainly in its earlier days, that the notion of inhuman treatment was, both in the Universal Declaration and in the Convention, a reflection of experiences in the second world war; and, that by it was meant treatment inhuman in the sense that it was totally abnormal, totally beyond any ordinary human practice or behaviour – the mass executions in gas ovens.

Later thinking claimed that this was in a way too narrow and restricted a view, and that inhuman treatment is really any severe pain or suffering, either physical or mental, imposed deliberately and unnecessarily. That is only, of course, a very rough description, and "unnecessary" excludes only medical treatment. The Economic, Social and Cultural Rights Covenant goes into the questions of scientific or medical experiments, which may of course involve pain and suffering, and in particular of whether it is legitimate that people should consent to their own ill-treatment for these purposes.

It would be generally agreed that torture is not essentially different in kind from inhuman treatment, being really severe ill-treatment for some specific purpose, usually the extraction of information. Here I think a real problem lies, in the application of this kind of prohibition, either in the Convention or the parallel United Nations Covenants. It is the problem of ill-treatment of prisoners or detainees for the purpose of obtaining information. Ill-treatment, of course, even in the form of a mere technical assault, will normally be punishable under domestic law. But what we are concerned with here is the operation of the Convention and Covenants in protecting individuals against this kind of ill treatment. The interrogation of detainees, whether they are political detainees or criminally charged or convicted, or prisoners of war, demands attention. Whether the interrogation is by security services, civil or military, or of prisoners captured during hostilities, I venture to say there are circumstances in which ill-treatment for purposes of obtaining information is virtually inevitable. It is certainly widespread in practice and I do not think that the Convention and Covenants have entirely faced this fact. When I say such ill-treatment is inevitable, I do not of course mean that it is therefore justified. But I was surprised to read a little time ago some statements in a book entitled *War and or Survival*. Admittedly with great caution, the author expressed the view that there could be circumstances in which torture or severe ill-treatment of prisoners of war might be justified. He limited it by saying that the information sought must be of critical importance, that any ill-treatment must be specifically sanctioned by some higher authority, and that it should be subject to some possible form of review. I would like to say that I do not think that the author was recommending this, but he was saying that this is a kind of argument that might be put forward in justification of a practice which is probably inevitable. My own view is that it would be a great mistake to attempt to formulate any such rule as the author suggests, and that the prohibition must remain absolute. Once you formulate a permissive rule you fall below a certain threshold and practice would get quite out of control.

On the contrary, the prohibitions in the Convention and Covenant need strengthening. It is true that the Prisoners-of-War Convention, the Geneva Convention of 1949, in Articles 13 and 17 dealing with the interrogation of prisoners, enunciated the old rule that the prisoner of war is only obliged to give his name, rank and number and there is a specific provision that he is not to be subjected to any ill-treatment or pressure to obtain information from him. So that Convention, at least, enunciated a clear rule. But the problem arises also with security services which may be operating in situations not unlike or close to that of war; they may have a strong sense of a protective function, that they are really defending their side or the community against hostile, devious and dangerous people – as they see them – and that they must urgently get needed information to perform this function adequately. You may add to that even hatred and fear of certain detainees.

A second feature is that there is very little higher control. One of the weaknesses, and grave disadvantages perhaps, of security services is that they too often stand outside the ordinary administrative system, whether of military administration in the broad sense, or the normal civil administration. This lack of higher control, and particularly the lack of public means of control, gives them certainly great power. Attempts then to protect detainees in this situation depend a great deal on the problem of proof. It is because in the ill-treatment of prisoners of war, or of other political detainees who are detained by security or even ordinary police, there is in the nature of the situation an absence or at least great difficulty in securing corroborative evidence. You have also a quite different complication in that in some situations the detainees' colleagues or supporters may have strong political interest in discrediting the security services, or in showing that the government it acts for is an illegal government.

Now, these are elements which do not normally arise in the investigation of ordinary crime, and create great difficulties for any international body trying to investigate allegations of torture or ill-treatment. The problem of proof must be tackled in a way that is both workable and will stand the test of criticism, including that by the government authority involved. Of the various reports that we have had in recent years from a number of countries, it is not sufficient to say that they can be disregarded, that they are just newspaper stories. This, of course, is not at all sufficient, but there still may be exaggeration, false rumours, and even, as I have said, a propaganda element. Therefore, in trying to operate the Convention or Covenants effectively, a strict standard of proof has to be applied; that is to say, an international body will achieve very little if it can do no better, or if it can maintain no better standards of inquiry, than other people whose means of investigation may be in various ways limited. A journalist may visit a country and do his best to check evidence, and indeed he may succeed and his story may be perfectly good, but he may be subject to limitations under which he cannot be expected to maintain the standards of proof that the Convention or Covenants require. Similarly, when Members of Parliament visit countries and, after talking to a few people, declare themselves satisfied that allegations of ill-treatment are entirely unfounded, it is not a proper method of inquiry. I would say the same of the Stockholm Conference on the investigation of war crimes in Viet Nam. Whatever the purposes of that Conference, and whether they are worthy or not, its methods fall below the acceptable standards of proof. In sum, an international body will only achieve any useful result – and it may not even achieve that – if it applies standards of proof beyond a reasonable doubt. This is a good and workable test, though it may be that in its application by an international body to a number of allegations a firm conclusion will be reached about only a few. It is more important for international protection to come to that result in the end than to have a vaguer conclusion about a large number of cases. By a reasonable doubt I would understand a doubt for which good reason can be given.

I come now to a third area, which is perhaps the more significant area in the operation of the Convention, namely its rules concerning detention. The Convention says in Article 5 that everyone has the right to liberty and security of person; it then lays down a number of conditions in which people may be detained in accordance with law and following procedures prescribed by law. Although these of course themselves form exceptions to the broad principle of liberty and security of person, they nevertheless are not open to any other exceptions. In other words, they have to be distinguished from those provisions concerning, for example, freedom of information, which are subject to a number of exceptions, such as legislation in the interests of public order or national security. But the provisions of Article 5 are to be observed in all circumstances unless of course a country derogates generally from the provisions of the Convention, or from some of its provisions, under Article 15. Certain derogations by the United Kingdom Government in respect of Northern Ireland have been maintained for a number of years. The detention provisions in Article 5 raise three practical issues which we may now examine.

The first concerns the meaning of the expression "security" of a person. It is perhaps rather strange that in applications to the Commission over sixteen years this has never been analysed or indeed very much discussed. By a general rule of interpretation, as the word is there – and it is certainly different in sense from "liberty" – some meaning must be given to it. It may be suggested that "liberty" in Article 5 really means a physical "liberty" – the rights not to be physically detained, not to be locked up in one way or another, of freedom of movement – and that "security" belongs to the same order of ideas. I do not find that entirely convincing. I do not think it is very easy to give a purely physical meaning to "security" when it is set side by side with "liberty". There are possibly two issues where its real meaning might have to be determined. One is over passports and the other is perhaps more widely over citizenship generally. As you may know, the East African Asians seeking to enter and stay in this country have made applications to the European Commission, and when the cases were admitted, they were admitted in part around this point; for the question may be asked whether or not citizenship involves in some respects security of person. It is perhaps surprising how vague in law the right of entry of a citizen to his own country often is. I believe that, as far as the law of this country goes, there is no rule of positive law to which I can appeal if I land at Dover as a United Kingdom citizen born in this country and claim right of entry. I suppose that refusal of entry must involve at least notional detention, and that in that case there would be no answer to an order of *habeas corpus*.

In some countries, too, you will find actual provisions of law that deny the right of entry to citizens in certain circumstances. So the right of entry of a citizen to his own country is not as clear perhaps as people sometimes suppose, or as it should be, under the laws of the particular countries.

Another area of detention which is troublesome in attempts to apply the Convention is that covered by the provisions in Article 5 (1) e for the detention of "vagrants (vagabonds)" and the detention of people of what the Convention calls "unsound mind (aliénés)". The Convention does not qualify the term "vagrant" in any way and, provided the detention of the vagrant is according to law, there is nothing contrary to the Convention in his detention. But this can, in a number of modern contexts, lead to difficulties and to a certain gap, if you like, in the effectiveness of the Convention. In some countries, Belgium for instance, the detention of the vagrant may be for long periods of time, certainly years. Further, it may be ordered by magistrates acting in a kind of administrative capacity, where the judicial process is not very visible. This issue has now been in part determined by the European Court of Human Rights.[1]

Again, from a practical point of view, the Convention provision on detention of people of unsound mind is difficult to administer,

[1] de Wilde, Ooms and Versyp Cases: Judgement (June 18 1971)

if a complaint is made in regard to it. They may be in some ways very acute and the account they may give of their treatment or their detention may be in many ways very convincing. But if, on the other hand, it is found that the order for their detention has been made by a court on medical advice or after inquiry by an expert commission, it is difficult to see how it can be challenged. This can be an important issue, as we see from the forms of abuse of it, which are dangerous.

The last kind of detention I shall mention is detention on remand. This has been a major problem under the European Convention. It is perhaps not often realised how long in some countries, that are parties to the Convention, a person may be detained on remand. There have been applications to the European Commission where the applicant has been detained for as long as three years; and periods of detention from one to two years are by no means infrequent. In a recent application from a detainee on remand, charged with war crimes, the length of detention was seven and a half years. In order to understand a little how this comes about, one has to note the differences in the procedure of criminal investigation. In this country we have what is generally called an accusatorial system under which, once a *prima facie* case is established, and the prosecuting authority is satisfied that there is a case to answer, then the matter can go fairly directly to a court where the charge is determined. As you know, the periods of detention pending trial are limited in this country, in particular under the Assizes Act 1889, so that the effective limit is around six months; I believe that in Scotland it is 210 days. Again as you know the ordinary periods of detention for various reasons, such as the over-burdening of the courts, are becoming in practice extended, giving cause for public complaint. I should perhaps mention here that one of the quickest operators is Sweden, where the average period of detention on remand appears to be under thirty days. But in some European countries, particularly Austria, the procedure is inquisitorial, in which a great deal of the burden of establishing the evidence supporting a criminal charge is given to an investigating judge. His task will be to interrogate witnesses, including of course the suspect himself, examine documentary evidence, and in the later stages at which the suspect has become the accused the investigatory procedure still continues. The situations where the charge is complex, as in a series of financial frauds, or evasions of import or export controls, the investigators *may* be faced with the need to assemble a vast mass of evidence, obtained at home and abroad; there may also be a legal requirement that every possible charge must be brought; in other words, if the accused has committed ten offences, every one of those offences must be charged. So, these complexities of procedure, which in many cases make the preliminary investigation very lengthy in practice. The detainee on remand may apply to the court in Austria every three months to ask for release pending trial on or without bail. But it is not often granted, in face of argument made of the danger of flight, covering of evidence, and so on. So what is in issue here is not simply a number of cases or individual instances in which a breach of the Convention is alleged, but the whole system; in other words, it is not a question simply of adjusting the claims of the individual applicant or conceivably giving him some form of compensation, or even securing his release pending trial. What is at issue is the whole method of administering criminal justice, and this may be much more difficult for a country to modify. So where the Convention provides that the person detained on suspicion is to be tried within a reasonable time or released pending trial, there can be great difficulty in coming to a conclusion, given the character of a particular system, as to what is a reasonable time.

A number of the provisions in the Conventions and Covenants appear right and just, but their application often contains many hidden difficulties, and I have asked myself how much thought has been given, in the drafting of the UN Civil and Political Rights Covenant and of the machinery for their enforcement, to the purely practical problem of dealing with applications that might be brought to the proposed Human Rights Committee on a world scale? I think there are at least two immediate problems that occur. One is that of language, and to deal with applications, even in the European context, can sometimes be slow and difficult from the language point of view, and on a world basis there would be here immense difficulties and delays in even preparing the applications for consideration by the Committee. The second problem, which I have just outlined, is that of the often wide differences of practice, the practices being not obviously indefensible in themselves. I cannot easily see how, even if a small number of countries accepted or recognised the right of individual petition, the Human

Rights Committee as it is organised under the Covenant would not be overwhelmed. I would only add here that the right to live and be free, to judge by the number of applications that have come to the Commission in sixteen years, are important, and are frequently invoked in people's minds.

I would suggest that the right to live and be free are central articles of the Convention and Covenants, and I believe that these rights are more likely to be protected effectively on the international plane on a regional basis, as they are in Europe and under the Inter-American Convention.

7. *The Legal Protection of Human Rights - National and International*

© PROFESSOR SIR HUMPHREY WALDOCK

Every legal right of the individual is by definition an interest which in greater or lesser degree has the protection of the law. The protection is in the first instance against the violation of his rights by other individuals; and this is true of what we consider as human rights no less than of other rights. Life, liberty and security of his person, peaceful enjoyment of possessions, respect for private life, freedom of thought, conscience and religion, of expression, assembly and association, for example, are all rights the secure enjoyment of which depends on other individuals being effectively restrained by law from violating them.

Thus, it is in a complex network of provisions of the criminal and civil law that what we conceive of as "human rights and fundamental freedoms" find their basic guarantees in relation to other members of the community. Moreover, since one man's right or freedom used to excess may mean the destruction or impairment of that of others, these provisions seek to find the just balance between man and man and to draw a line between an individual's use and abuse of his rights and freedoms. Such, for example, is conspicuously the case with the provisions of our law concerning defamation, nuisance, negligence, public meetings and processions in public places. Indeed, the very concept of the reasonable man, which is so characteristic of the many legal systems founded upon the common law, is an expression of that aspect of the legal protection of the rights and freedoms of the individual.

All this, you may say, is very elementary; it is what law itself is all about. You may even ask what it has to do with the subject of human rights which we usually think of as concerned with the protection of the individual against the arbitrary power of the state. But the events of recent years have forced upon our attention again and again the fact that the protection of the individual *vis a vis* his fellow man is no less vital to the enjoyment of his human rights and freedoms than his protection against the state. The multifarious problems which we refer to compendiously under the heading of pollution of the environment, the technological threat to man's privacy, sit-ins, demonstrations, race relations, kidnapping, hijacking, etc., are all matters which concern human rights and freedoms. The protection of the individual *vis à vis* his fellow men within his own community has been, and still largely is, considered as essentially the business of national law. In general, national law, more especially the law governing public order, contains the necessary panoply of rules to protect the rights of individuals; and today the problem in a mature democracy tends rather to be to find the appropriate balance in the application of these rules when rights come into conflict. That problem you can see illustrated by the modern sit-ins and demonstrations in the interest of good, or well-meaning or passionately believed-in causes. Those who take part in such incidents are not infrequently overriding the rights of other quite blameless members of the community and infringing prescriptions of the criminal law. But the law is applied flexibly in an attempt to find an acceptable balance between the rights of the community as a whole and the freedoms of conscience, thought and expression of those who demonstrate. The public, or a section of the public, may on this or that occasion feel that the executive or the courts have misjudged that balance; and there may sometimes be grounds for that feeling. However, we should never forget that what is at issue is not a matter simply between the offending individual and the authorities but also between citizen and citizen. Nor should we forget that many a dictator or ruthless political party has seized power unlawfully in the name of freedom, or social justice.

The Universal Declaration of Human Rights, both the United Nations Human Rights Covenants, the European and the Pan-American Human Rights Conventions all have a clause to the effect that nothing which they contain may be interpreted as implying for any state, group or person any right to engage in any activity or perform any act aimed at the destruction of any of the rights or freedoms for which it provides. Thus, rights or freedoms exercised for the purpose of destroying the rights or freedoms of others lose their legal protection under these instruments in so far as they are exercised for that purpose. Moreover, in a more general way these instruments all recognise expressly that the exercise of many of the rights and freedoms which they guarantee is subject to the restrictions considered necessary in a democratic society for the protection of the rights and freedoms of others. Some learned commentators on the European Convention indeed maintain that by implication it imposes a general obligation upon individuals, as well as upon states, to respect the rights and freedoms which its provisions guarantee.

In internal law human rights have in the past been viewed primarily as the protection of the individual against the power of the state. Our own law, by its development of the principles which form the basis of the Rule of Law, contributed much to the legal doctrines and to the legal techniques on which that protection is based in a free society. Since the American and French Revolutions many written constitutions have contained specific provisions protecting the fundamental rights and freedoms of the individual which in modern international instruments are classed as civil and political rights: life, liberty, security of the person, fair administration of justice and the great political and religious freedoms which characterise a free society. Today it is recognised that the classical rights and freedoms are not by themselves enough. Without a minimum of "social justice" – without, that is, a minimum of economic, social and cultural rights – the enjoyment of the classical rights and freedoms cannot be meaningful. Naturally, the recognition and legal protection of these rights is further advanced in the more developed states in which, however, they tend to be realised more through social and industrial legislation than through formal constitutional provisions. The Communist states and some of the newer states, are exceptions, for a number of these rights are formally proclaimed in their constitutions. But it is on the international plane – in such instruments as the United Nations Covenant on Economic, Social and Cultural Rights and the European Social Charter – that these rights have blossomed into a general legal concept.

The rights embraced in this new concept of human rights are somewhat different in kind from the classical civil and political rights. Their protection needs not negative restraints upon the state but the positive exercise of its powers to develop and distribute the nation's resources: in other words, the kind of legal measures which we associate with the welfare state. In due course they may find more specific recognition in national law as, for example, has freedom from economic and social discrimination in our own Race Relations Act. But their effective realisation depends on the economic and social policies of governments and parliaments even more than on legal provisions. I shall not therefore dwell on them now, though later I shall say a word about the international machinery devised for their protection.

Futhermore, important though economic, social and cultural rights may be to the full realisation of human personality, history and present experience alike show that their recognition and enjoyment are bound up with the protection of civil and political rights. Accordingly, it is on the latter that I shall now concentrate. I do so the more readily because the boundary between the exercise of civil and political rights and the needs of law and order is one of the prime issues of our day.

Any special protection of rights as human rights presupposes some identification of those rights by the law. In the United Kingdom this identification has been effected as much by the judges as by any legislative act. But in most modern states, as I said, the identification is found in a written constitution. Dicey considered that our constitutional rights and liberties are all the stronger for being derived from judge-made law rather than from constitutional guarantees; and he thought the very idea of written guarantees of our fundamental liberties to be "utterly alien to English modes of thought". This was in line with the emphasis which he placed on what he called "that inseparable connection between the means of enforcing a right and the right to be enforced". The Englishmen, he said, whose labours gradually framed our constitution, fixed their minds far more intently on providing remedies than upon any declaration of the Rights of Man or of Englishmen. "The Habeas Corpus Acts", he added, "declare no principle and define no rights, but they are for practical purposes worth a hundred constitutional articles guaranteeing individual liberty".

We may regretfully agree that all too often written constitutions have sooner or later been treated as scraps of paper. We may also endorse wholeheartedly Dicey's insistence upon the importance of the judiciary in the protection of human rights. But we are less sure today that we are better without a written constitution. The corollary of the unwritten character of our constitution, as Dicey himself insisted, is that Parliament is sovereign *over* the law, in the sense that it may at any time make or unmake any law whatever, and that whatever Parliament enacts the judges must apply. Simply in terms of law, therefore, human rights are wide open to violation by Parliament itself. Furthermore, under the Parliament Acts of 1911 and 1949, Parliament for this purpose means the House of Commons, subject only to a brief delaying power in the Lords; and the House of Commons in turn means the party with an effective majority in that chamber. Accordingly, and again simply in terms of law, there is nothing in our system to prevent a party from lawfully acquiring power through the ballot box and then playing fast and loose with human rights, more especially those of their opponents.

You may by now be beginning to suspect that it is something other than the law that provides the real guarantee of our liberties; and you would be right. Law can and must furnish the machinery for the effective realisation of human rights and of a truly free society. But the strength of the protection which any system of law can give to rights and freedoms depends in large measure on the social solidarity of the community which it serves and the place which law and the judiciary have in the social consciousness of the people. In other words, it is social forces behind the law, rather than the law itself, which form the guarantee of civil and political rights in a free society. Nevertheless, just as with a private transaction, so with a constitution, a well-designed legal framework may make a great deal of difference; and today some have ventured to ask whether we might not be safer with at least some written, "entrenched", provisions concerning our basic civil and political rights. Indeed, only yesterday the House of Lords was debating a Bill of Rights introduced by the Earl of Arran with that very object in view.[1]

It is not that any dramatic deterioration in the attitudes of our rulers and our political parties towards the rights and freedoms of the individual is to be expected. In our system the action of the judiciary is reinforced by restraints of other kinds upon the Government's exercise of its executive and legislative powers: the customs, procedures and privileges of Parliament, the individual Member's paternalistic right to take up the cudgels on behalf of an aggrieved constituent, question time in the House, the Ombuds-

[1] i.e. on Nov. 26th, 1970

man, our independent press, television and radio and a whole host
of associations, organisations and committees all over the country,
alert to act as watchdogs for particular interests or causes. Like
Gulliver, the Government is held down by a myriad of these fine
threads spun by the free spirit of our people over the centuries.
So long as this free spirit and the social solidarity of our people
remain, our character as a truly free society is unlikely to be
seriously endangered.

What Lord Arran and others fear is rather that under the pressure of its business Parliament, by ill-considered or inadvertent
legislation, or beguiled by bureaucrats' demands, or through sheer
excess of zeal for a supposed public interest, may pass laws that
nibble away the individual's fundamental rights. Within the limits
of judicial interpretation the courts may seek to reconcile such
laws with the individual's fundamental rights; but beyond that
they are powerless to do anything but apply them. Accordingly,
they have suggested the need for an entrenched statement of certain
rights and freedoms by reference to which our courts may control
the observance of human rights by Parliament itself.

Dicey himself stressed that the English system of rights and
remedies is in no way inconsistent with the existence of a written
constitution or of a constitutional declaration of rights; and he
pointed to the United States Constitution as embodying the
virtues of both systems. There the compatibility of ordinary laws
with the Constitution is subject to judicial control, while the
Constitution itself may be amended only through a special procedure. Today, the constitutions of some other states also embody
this double-banked system of guarantees of fundamental rights.
Whether such a system is desirable for us and, if so, whether it is
politically negotiable I must leave to you. But we live in times of
thrustful challenge to authority and of recourse to direct action
rather than to the recognised processes of change; and this may
be another reason why you may wish to ask yourself that question.

In fact, as I observed in Brussels some dozen years ago, the
United Kingdom Constitution does now have superimposed upon
it written guarantees of the classical civil rights and freedoms –
guarantees on the international plane in a legal instrument
operating within the larger framework of the Council of Europe.
I referred, of course, to the European Convention on Human
Rights. When I made that observation, the operation of those

guarantees was still wholly extraneous to the United Kingdom. Under our law a treaty, though binding upon us internationally, does not have the force of law here unless converted into United Kingdom law by Act of Parliament; and no such action had then, or has since, been taken with reference to the European Convention. Moreover, at that date the United Kingdom had agreed to answer before the organs of the Council of Europe for any violation of the Convention only upon complaint by another member state. She was indeed brought before the European Commission by Greece on two separate complaints concerning the actions of British authorities and forces in Cyprus during the emergency in 1956. But the application of the Convention was then for the United Kingdom a matter exclusively between states, and its guarantees remained something remote from our domestic law, from our judges and from our legal profession.

In 1966 the situation changed radically when the United Kingdom accepted the right of individuals to petition the European Commission under Article 25 of the Convention. True, the guarantees in the Convention can still not be applied by our judges. But our acceptance of Article 25 gave everyone within the jurisdiction of the United Kingdom, whether nationals or foreigners, that thing most prized by Dicey, a legal remedy: a remedy, maybe, before an international body, yet nonetheless a legal remedy. At once the guarantees in the Convention began to have meaning not only for individuals in this country but, no less important, for our legal profession. As to the latter, recourse to the Commission now forms part of the armoury of legal weapons potentially at the disposal of their clients. For many, it may still appear a somewhat esoteric weapon. But its use has been growing, as you will know from press references to the Kenya-Asians' cases and to the cases from Northern Ireland, including that of Miss Devlin.

I may, perhaps, add that the right of audience before the Commission is open to both branches of our legal profession, barristers and solicitors, as indeed also to academic lawyers.

Acceptance of the individual right of petition, if it has to that extent built a bridge between the guarantees of the European Convention and our legal system, has not made them part of it. In this respect, Eire, and the Scandinavian States, are in much the same position as ourselves, because in their case also there is no automatic incorporation of treaties in their domestic law. The

United Kingdom, like those States, believes that the rights and freedoms set forth in the Convention already find their full expression and protection in our domestic law. If on some point this belief should prove unfounded, our judges must nevertheless apply our domestic law in preference to the prescriptions of the European Convention, even if this may mean violating the latter. Within the margins of possible legal interpretation our judges may seek to reconcile the application of our law with the Convention. Beyond that, however, their loyalty is to our law, not to the Convention.

A different situation prevails in countries such as Belgium, Holland, Luxembourg, Germany, Austria, Italy and Turkey where, under certain conditions, treaties become part of the domestic law. In those countries the provisions of the Convention are applicable by the judiciary alongside the domestic law. But even then the status of the Convention as domestic law varies from country to country. In some it has the rank only of an ordinary statute, so that, while it prevails over any prior law, it will be over-ridden by any later statute inconsistent with it. In Austria, on the other hand, the Convention has now been given the rank of a constitutional provision and thus prevails over any later as well as prior *ordinary* statute. In Holland and Luxembourg the Convention, in so far as its provisions are self-executing, prevails over both prior and later statutes. But it seems that the Dutch courts do not take an extensive view of their power to control the legality of Parliamentary legislation, while in Luxembourg doubts have been entertained as to the self-executing character of the Convention. Cyprus and Malta are special cases in that the Constitutions themselves contain elaborate guarantees of human rights; and under the Cyprus Constitution the Convention, as a treaty, is also itself part of the domestic law. In some of these countries, notably Germany, Austria, Italy, Belgium and the Netherlands, the provisions of the Convention have not infrequently been invoked in litigation in the domestic courts.

Our acceptance of the individual right of petition, I said, added recourse to the European Commission to the armoury of legal weapons for the protection of human rights in the United Kingdom. But I must not leave you with any wrong ideas about the nature of that remedy or its place in the legal scheme of things. The guarantees of the Convention are, I emphasised, superimposed upon our Constitution. In other words, they are a supplement to, not a substitution for, the legal protection afforded by our own law. Article 26 provides categorically that the Commission may only deal with the matter after all domestic remedies have been exhausted according to the generally recognised rules of international law. In substance this means that the individual must first exhaust any legal remedies which exist in the domestic system of the state concerned and which are to be considered as potentially effective and adequate remedies in regard to the matters of which he complains. If none such exist or recourse to those which exist would obviously be futile, he may go at once to the Commission. Otherwise he must make full use of the available domestic remedies up to the highest tribunal. The purpose of this general rule of international law is to safeguard the right of the state to do justice to persons within its jurisdiction through its own laws and its own courts. Only when these have failed to remedy a violation of one of the rights guaranteed in the Convention does the international machinery come into play. Without some such division of competence between international and domestic tribunals there might, as you can imagine, be a chaotic confusion of legal proceedings.

Recourse to the Commission is therefore a remedy in reserve – a long stop to catch the failures of the domestic system. Does this mean that it is too belated a remedy to be effective? In the more exceptional case where the domestic system affords no relevant remedy, recourse may be had to the Commission without delay. In other cases, since the international tribunal must deal with the matter after the closure of the domestic proceedings, it necessarily comes into play more belatedly than the local courts. The international remedy cannot, therefore, normally have the speedy character of a writ of *habeas corpus*. But the Convention itself presupposes that each state shall provide an adequate system of legal remedies and tribunals for the administration of justice and the protection of the liberty of the person. Indeed, Article 5 specifically includes among the rights guaranteed by the Convention the right of everyone deprived of his liberty by arrest or detention to take proceedings by which the lawfulness of his detention shall be decided speedily by a court and his release ordered if the detention is not lawful. The alleged failure of a state to provide such proceedings may itself be made a ground of action before the Commission, as happened in the Belgian Vagrancy Cases now before the European Court. It follows that in the nature of things the value of the international remedy tends rather to be in putting an end to a continuing violation of human rights or in affording redress for one that has already been completed.

Here I must underline that a state is answerable before the European Commission and Court only for acts or omissions of its authorities which constitute violations of the Convention; it is not answerable for illegalities or arbitrary acts which are not of such a character as to bring them within the four corners of any of the particular rights and freedoms guaranteed in the Convention. Amongst those rights is a right to the fair administration of justice within a reasonable time, by an independent and impartial tribunal established by law. But this does not mean that every error of law or fact committed by a judge constitutes a violation of the Convention. Provided that the rules and standards of "fair trial" have been observed, the ultimate decision is outside the control of the Convention, unless it establishes a situation which is itself in conflict with the Convention. The Commission and the Court are not, in short, some form of general Super-Supreme Court of Appeal for Europe.

The Convention has proved significant notably in two ways. First, it has been the means of uncovering particular defects in the legal systems of this or that country presenting a potential threat to human rights. Austria's appellate procedure in criminal cases, for example, contained one feature which the Commission considered to be incompatible with the principle of the "equality of arms" between the accused and the prosecution. The Austrian Government settled a large block of cases which raised this point by undertaking to amend its law and to set up a special procedure for reviewing the sentences of the individuals involved. Again, in the *De Becker* case Belgium's post-war laws dealing with collaborators, understandably severe, were found by the Commission on certain points to go beyond what could be considered admissible restrictions upon freedom of expression. The Commission referred the case to the European Court for decision, but meanwhile the Belgian Government introduced amending legislation which removed the offending elements from the laws in question and, De Becker having withdrawn his claim, the case did not proceed to judgment. More recently, in the *Delcourt* case, the compatibility of the rôle in criminal cases of the Procureur Général of Belgium's Cour de Cassation, her highest tribunal, with the principle of the "equality of arms" underwent the close scrutiny of both the Commission and the Court before being finally upheld. You yourselves may have seen references to the *Belgian Linguistic* cases, where the Court concluded that on one point in certain areas the Belgian legislation did not respect the principle of non-discrimination in the enjoyment of the right to education; and that on another point some possible applications of the legislation might give rise to infringements of that principle. I say nothing of the cases against the United Kingdom which are now before the Commission and therefore *sub judice*. But I may mention two cases in which points in our procedural system were brought into question before the Commission, though unsuccessfully. In one, the complainant attacked the practice of the House of Lords of giving no reasons when refusing leave to appeal; in the other the complainant attacked the procedure of the Court of Criminal Appeal when dealing with applications for leave to appeal. Both cases required a nice appreciation of the compatibility of the procedure in question with the "fair trial" provisions of Article 6 of the Convention.

Another, and broader, example of the importance of the Convention in regard to defects of system is the series of cases which have come before the Commission and the Court concerning length of detention on remand before trial and the length of criminal proceedings. In this country we ourselves are preoccupied with the law's delays in dealing with the mounting load of crime, and we look to the reorganisation of our courts system resulting from the Beeching report as a solution to or reduction of those delays. But under our accusatorial system we measure delays in terms of months rather than years. Article 5 of the Convention gives to everyone arrested or detained on suspicion of having committed an offence the right to *"trial within a reasonable time or to release pending trial"*. Clearly, it would be inappropriate for me to express any opinion as to what length of delays under our system might eventually be considered incompatible with that right; for the question may possibly one day be before the Court. The cases so far considered by the Commission and the Court have all come from countries with the inquisitorial system of criminal procedure, under which the investigation of the case is the responsibility of an examining magistrate rather than of the prosecution. The pre-trial proceedings are, thus, in some degree part of the process of "trial", and under this system very considerable periods of time may elapse between the arrest or detention of an accused and the final hearing and judgment in open court. In some cases also, for example in complicated financial frauds, the period of actual detention on remand, without release on bail, may be very prolonged. A Chamber of the Court has already given judgment in four such cases where the periods of detention varied between two and three years, two of the cases being from Austria and two from Germany. In brief, the Chamber found the periods of detention without release to have been unreasonable in two of the cases and not unreasonable in the other two. It determined the compatibility of the detentions with the requirements of Article 5 by reference to the circumstances of each case and in particular to considerations such as the risks of flight, the length of sentence to be expected if the case were proved, etc. Some continental lawyers seem to consider that the Chamber allowed continental conceptions of criminal trial to be in some degree overborne by the speedier conceptions of the common law. I was not myself a member of that Chamber, but I doubt if you will find much evidence for such a view in the judgments in those cases. What the Chamber clearly did do was to decide that, under any system of criminal trial, there is some limit to the length of detention, without release on bail, which is acceptable under the Convention. Other cases may be on the way, and I must leave the matter there. I may, however, add that in 1964 the Federal Republic of Germany amended its Criminal Procedure so as to provide that remand in custody should not exceed six months except in special circumstances.

The other way in which the Convention has proved significant is in the supervision which the Commission and Court may exercise over a government's recourse to emergency powers, should the matter be brought before the Commission. Here you come to the very core of the legal protection of human rights. In time of emergency a government must have the right to invoke special powers and, if need be, suspend some of the normal guarantees of fundamental rights. We ourselves have our Emergency Powers Act and nearly every modern constitution contains provision for declaring a state of siege or suspending constitutional guarantees in certain circumstances. Yet, in times of internal tension these powers are wide open to abuse by a government determined to suppress its opponents. Moreover, control of the exercise of these powers through internal legal procedures is apt to be defeated by the very nature of the emergency powers. For this reason international supervision and control of recourse to emergency powers involving derogations from human rights assumes a particular importance. So it is that Article 15 of the European Convention seeks to hedge around the use of such powers with restrictions. It admits recourse to them only "in time of war or other public emergency threatening the life of the nation", and it allows the state concerned to take measures derogating from the rights in the Convention only "to the extent strictly required by the exigencies of the situation" and to the extent that "they are not inconsistent with other obligations under international law". Indeed, it wholly forbids derogations from certain articles. Moreover, it requires any state resorting to the right of derogation under the Article to keep the Secretary-General of the Council of Europe fully informed of the measures which it has taken and the reasons for them. Analogous provisions appear in the United Nations Covenants and in the Pan-American Convention.

In Europe we have seen the value of Article 15, if we have also seen the political limits to the effectiveness of international control. Recourse to emergency powers has not been infrequent. Our Government has invoked Article 15 with reference to Northern Ireland, Cyprus and certain other former colonial territories; and the Eire Government has in the past done so with reference to Irish Republican Army activities in its territory. Some years ago there appeared also to be use of such powers by Turkey, but the matter was never raised under Article 15. Then, quite recently, you have the situation in Greece. Accordingly, we do know something of the impact of the Convention in situations of emergency, and to me the most significant point is that, when such a situation is brought before the Commission, you have at once a quite different atmosphere in which the government's emergency powers are operated. This was certainly so, for example, in the case of Cyprus, when the emergency was very grave and when strong legislation had been introduced, including such measures as corporal punishment, detention without trial, collective fines on communities, etc. Greece brought a case before the Commission challenging the compatibility of these measures with the Convention, and the whole situation at once began in large degree to come under the supervision of the Commission. Written and oral proceedings followed and the result was a noticeable easing of the understandably drastic emergency legislation of the Cyprus Government. Some of the measures, in particular corporal punishment and collective fines, were either withdrawn or no longer persisted with.

In the case of Eire the emergency situation in that country was brought before the Commission by an individual. Lawless, a member of the Irish Republican Army, complained of having been detained without trial under special legislation introduced under emergency powers to deal with the situation. At once the checks and controls provided in Article 15 came into play and, although the Commission in fact upheld the measures complained of by Lawless, the value of the international supervision provided by the Convention was again illustrated. Even in the recent case of Greece, it may fairly be concluded that the mere fact that a number of European governments instituted proceedings before the Commission exercised a material influence in mitigating the measures taken by the Greek Government in respect of some individuals. Unfortunately, however, the case of Greece illustrates the political limits, as well as the potentialities, of any system of international guarantees of human rights. The question is not one merely of establishing effective legal machinery of supervision but also of obtaining the compliance of the government with the resulting findings of the international organs concerned. For Greece, as you know, denounced the Convention and withdrew from the Council of Europe. But this episode, although it shows the political limits which may at present exist upon effective international protection of human rights, shows nothing more. Certainly, it does nothing to indicate the ineffectiveness of a human rights convention among democratic states who adhere to democracy.

If I have focused your attention on the European Convention, this is because it is an example of a system of international protection which is in active operation and of the working of which much is already known. More recently, as you will be aware, the United Nations has produced its own Human Rights Covenants, designed to be of world-wide application: one on Economic and

Social Rights and the other on Civil and Political Rights. The rights sought to be protected by these Covenants are somewhat wider in scope than those covered by the European Convention and the European Social Charter. On the other hand, the machinery of international supervision which they provide, although significant, is not so rigorous as that afforded by the European Convention. Moreover, a considerable number of states must ratify or accede to the Covenants before they come into force and, having regard to the nature of the obligations which they contain, it may be some years before the required number of ratifications and accessions is forthcoming. The states of the Council of Europe, I may add, are in principle anxious to ratify the United Nations Covenants; but the coexistence and overlapping of the two systems of international protection of human rights do pose complex problems for them. Meanwhile, the Organisation of American States has also drawn up its own convention for the protection of human rights and freedoms, modelled in large degree on the European Convention but embracing a wider range of rights.

Finally, in order that my emphasis on the European Convention may not distort the picture for you, I must briefly remind you of some of the other contributions made by international law to the protection of human rights. The Geneva Conventions for mitigating human suffering in time of war have a long history, as have also conventions for abolishing slavery, traffic in women and children and traffic in drugs. The International Labour Organisation, which is now fifty years old, has established a truly impressive body of international labour law and standards of conduct for the protection of the rights of workers, backed up by various systems of supervision and control through its organs. The United Nations itself has drawn up a number of significant Declarations and Conventions on particular aspects of human rights, such as the rights of women and racial discrimination. It has also taken significant initiatives in promoting international action for the protection of the environment. As to the gravest human rights problem of all, the extreme poverty of large sections of the world's population, numerous organisations both universal and regional are in diverse ways seeking to mitigate, if not solve, it.

Ideals of human rights and social justice may make us impatient. But the political, economic and legal problems are formidable, and it is only by unceasing efforts to educate public opinion and unremitting attempts to push the frontiers of international protection ever a little further that real progress can be made. In the field of human rights, as in other parts of international law, the problem is not one merely of drawing up agreements but of making them effective. Here, above all, you may feel sure that Europe has taken the lead and shown the way to an effective legal system for the international guarantee of human rights and freedoms.

8. War and Human Rights

© MISS J. A. C. GUTTERIDGE

Is it not anomalous to speak of human rights in the context of war? If one of the fundamental human rights is, as stated in Article 6 of the International Covenant on Civil and Political Rights, "the inherent right to life", is it not unrealistic to speak of the protection of human rights in situations of violence aimed at the destruction of human life?

If it is indeed true, as was alleged in a letter to *The Times*[1] about the My Lai Court Martial, that "the Laws and Usages of war . . . have long been *de facto* obsolete", the subject of this lecture would be of academic interest only. But the picture is not as dark as this. A Resolution unanimously adopted at the International Conference on Human Rights held at Teheran in the spring of 1968, whilst affirming that "peace is the underlying condition for the full observation of human rights and war is their negation", noted that armed conflicts continue to plague humanity and expressed the conviction that even during the period of armed conflict humanitarian principles must prevail. In other words, even if no government can in practice renounce recourse to force, strict limits must be placed on its use both in peace and in war. To hold that the Laws and Usages of War are obsolete is to discredit the whole idea of restraint in the use of force. Like the writer of another recent letter to *The Times*,[2] "I can think of nothing more likely to add to human misery".

Setting aside a war the aim of which is the total extermination of a people and which constitutes the international crime of genocide under Article 1 of the Genocide Convention, and bearing in mind that the circumstances and weapons of modern war have blurred the old distinction between combatant and non-combatant, it is still true to say that the purpose of a war or other armed conflict is the destruction of an entity – an enemy state or government – and not the destruction of individuals who for one reason

[1] *The Times*, April 7, 1971.

[2] *Ibid.*, April 4, 1971

99

or another play no part in the conflict and who are in the literal sense of the phrase *hors de combat* – outside the conflict.

This distinction was first made by Rousseau in his *Contrat Social*, which was published in 1762. He then said: "The object of war being the destruction of the enemy state, one has the right to kill its defenders only when they have weapons in their hands, but immediately they put them down and surrender, thus ceasing to be enemies or agents of the enemy, they once more become ordinary men and one no longer has any right to their life."

This view, which Rousseau stated "flowed from the nature of things and was founded on reason", was in advance of his time. Even in national armies the casualties of the battlefield received little respect or protection. As late as the Crimean War, "The men who had stormed the heights of Alma, charged with the Light Brigade at Balaclava and fought the grim battle against overwhelming odds at Inkerman, perished of hunger and neglect."[3] It is, therefore, not surprising that the concept that those outside the conflict by reason of wounds or sickness should be respected and protected had very little effect on the conduct of belligerents in the hundred years that elapsed between the publication of Rousseau's *Contrat Social* and the first Geneva Convention of 1864.

It is therefore unexpected to find that it is in the context of war that rules for the protection of individuals legally binding upon states are formulated in the middle of the nineteenth century. These rules are a very early departure from the concept that international law is concerned only with the rights and duties of states, and a movement towards the recognition of human rights in international law.

The first Geneva Convention for the Amelioration of the Conditions of the Wounded and Sick in Armies in the Field was the direct result of the experiences of a Swiss citizen, Henri Dunant, who, influenced by Florence Nightingale's work in the Crimea, was present at the Battle of Solferino in 1859. At that battle 38,000 officers and soldiers were killed or wounded within fifteen hours. Many of the wounded could have been saved if there had been any arrangements between the belligerents for removing them from the field of battle and caring for them. In 1861 Hans Durand published a pamphlet called *Souvenir de Solferino*; the

[3] C. Woodham-Smith, *Florence Nightingale*, p. 203.

publication of this led directly, as he had wished, both to the formation of national societies to assist the medical service of armies in the field, and to the endorsement of such assistance as "un principe conventionnel et sacré" by the governments of states. In 1863 a conference at which sixteen states were represented founded the organisation known thenceforward as the Red Cross.

In a "voeu" annexed to its Resolutions this Conference called for the "neutralisation" of medical personnel of armies in the field, and of the wounded themselves. In 1864, in pursuance of this "voeu", a diplomatic conference drew up the first of what have come to be known as the "Red Cross" Conventions. This Convention consisted of ten Articles; these provided in short that military ambulances and hospitals were to be recognised as neutral and, as such, protected and respected; that military wounded or sick must be cared for whatever their country; and that wounded who were captured must be sent home if incapable of further service.

The 1864 Convention, it has been well said,[4] consecrated the principle that the wounded and sick of armies in the field must, from the moment they become harmless and without defence, be respected and cared for without distinction of nationality. This was the concept implied by the term "neutral" – a term hitherto applied in the Law of War only to states – and when the 1864 Convention was first revised in 1906 this concept was spelt out in an Article which said expressly that "Members of the armed forces who are wounded and sick shall be respected and protected in all circumstances".

Thus, from 1864 onwards, it was accepted that there was a category of persons whose rights as human beings must be respected and protected in time of war, and that to ensure such respect and protection was the duty of states under international law. To quote from the Commentary on the Wounded and Sick Convention prepared by the International Red Cross in 1952, "C'était . . . l'avènement des idées morales touchant à la personne humaine dans la sphère des intérêts d'Etats".[5]

[4] Pictet, *Commentaire sur les Conventions de Genève du 12 août* 1949, Vol. I, p. 9.

[5] Pictet, *op. cit.*, p. 9.

The concept enshrined in the 1864 Convention began to influence other developments in the Law of War. In 1868 the Declaration of St Petersburg expressly prohibited the employment in wars among the parties of any projectile of a weight below 400 grammes which was either explosive or charged with ful- minating or inflammable substances. It is, however, the preamble to the Declaration which is of particular interest in the present context. It proclaimed, *inter alia*, that the progress of civilisation should have the effect of alleviating as much as possible the calamities of war; that the only legitimate objective of war is to weaken the military forces of the enemy, and that this objective would be exceeded by the employment of weapons which uselessly aggravated the sufferings of disabled men, and made their death inevitable.

In 1874 an international conference held in Brussels drew up a draft Declaration on the Laws and Customs of War, and although this was not ratified it was the genesis of the Fourth Hague Convention of 1899 on the Laws and Customs of War on Land and the Regulations annexed to that Convention. Furthermore, some of its principles began to find their way into manuals and instructions issued to national armies.

The Hague Regulations, as is pointed out in the recent report on Respect for Human Rights in Armed Conflict presented to the General Assembly by the Secretary-General of the United Nations,[6] "for several decades remained the main norms governing the humanitarian aspects of the law of armed conflict". Further- more, as was stated in the judgement of the Nuremberg Tribunal of 10 October 1946: "By 1939 the rules of land warfare laid down in the 1907 Convention had been recognised by all civilised nations and were regarded as declaratory of the laws and customs of war".

The Hague Regulations, both as adopted in 1899 and revised in 1907, contained in Section I rules for the treatment of prisoners of war which were the genesis of the later Prisoners of War Conven- tion. Section III of the Regulations contained what has been described[7] as "the nucleus of a system of protection for inhabitants of occupied territories". This section of the Regulations is thus the forerunner of the considerably later Convention relative to the

[6] UN Doc. A/7720.

[7] A/7720 para. 47.

Protection of Civilian Persons in Time of War. Although eight of the fourteen articles in this section – entitled "Military Authority over a Hostile State" – concerned the protection of property rather than the protection of individuals, it did provide expressly that family honour and rights, individual life and private property, as well as religious convictions and worship, must be respected.

The impetus given by the 1864 "Wounded and Sick" Convention and by the Hague Conventions of 1899 and 1907 to the recognition of the existence of certain human rights in time of war and the protection of those rights was maintained. The "Wounded and Sick" Convention has been revised three times – in 1906, in 1929 and in 1949. Its principles were adapted to maritime warfare in one of the Hague Conventions of 1899, which was revised in 1907 and became known as the Xth Hague Convention. That Convention was in turn revised by the 1949 Geneva Convention for the Amelioration of the Condition of Wounded, Sick and Shipwrecked Members of Armed Forces at Sea. The protection afforded by the Hague Regulations to prisoners of war was considerably extended in 1929 when a separate Prisoners of War Convention, which was stated in Article 89 thereof to be complementary to Chapter 2 of Section I of the Hague Regulations, was adopted in the light of the experience of the First World War. The Prisoners of War Convention was again revised in 1949 to remedy gaps and deficiencies in it found to exist in the Second World War.

Another development in the Law of War, intended to reduce the barbarity of modern warfare, and so relevant in the context of human rights, was the adoption in 1925 of the Geneva Protocol prohibiting amongst the parties thereto the use of "asphyxiating poisons or other gases and of all analogous liquid, materials or devices".

As I have already indicated, the experiences of the Second World War disclosed many gaps in the protection of the victims of war. Although considerable protection was afforded to prisoners of war by the 1929 Convention when both belligerents were parties to it, the appalling experiences of Russian prisoners of war in German hands, and of all prisoners of war in Japanese hands, illustrated what could happen in situations to which the 1929 Convention was not considered to apply. Furthermore, the occupation of a number of countries in Europe and in Asia disclosed how inadequate was the protection afforded by existing rules of international law to civilians in the hands of an occupying power. It was not only gross instances of reprisals against civilians – for example the destruction of the village of Lidice and the slaughter of all its male inhabitants – but also, for example, the conditions under which civilians in enemy hands were interned, and the widespread deportation of civilians from occupied territory, which highlighted the need for further and much more adequate protection of the civilian population.

In the light of experiences of the kind to which I have briefly referred, four new Conventions were drawn up in Geneva in 1949 at a diplomatic conference on the basis of texts already prepared under the aegis of the International Red Cross. Three of the 1949 Geneva Conventions, as I have already indicated, were revisions of existing Conventions; the fourth was an entirely new Convention relative to the Protection of Civilian Persons in Time of War.

These four instruments – although each of them can be acceded to separately – are grouped together under the title of the Conventions on the Protection of the Victims of War. This essential unity is emphasised by the fact that there are at the beginning of each Convention a group of articles common to all four Conventions. In the context of the protection of human rights in time of war these "common articles" are of particular importance, particularly as they are relevant to the question I propose to examine towards the end of this lecture – the question of whether existing rules of international law and, in particular, the 1949 Geneva Conventions, are adequate to ensure the protection of human rights in armed conflicts at the present time.

I propose therefore to examine the "common articles" in some detail. Under the first of them, the Parties "undertake to respect and to ensure respect for the Convention in all circumstances"; this, for instance, would make it impossible for a Party to argue that the Prisoners of War Convention was not applicable in a war of aggression to members of the aggressor's armed forces. The second "common article" provides that each Convention as a whole applies "to all cases of declared war or of any other armed conflict which may arise between two or more of the High Contracting Parties, even if the state of war is not recognised by one of them". This provision was inserted because there had been in recent times circumstances in which opposing states were engaged in armed conflict on a large scale, but one or both of them had disclaimed the intention to bring into being a state of war. For instance, in the conflict between China and Japan in the years immediately preceding the Second World War, China contended that she was only defending her territory against invasion and Japan claimed that she was simply conducting military operations for the purpose of protecting her nationals.

A further provision in Article 2 is that although one of the Powers in conflict may not be a party to the Convention, the Powers who are Parties remain bound by it in their mutual relations, and furthermore are bound by the Convention in relation to a non-party, if the latter "accepts and applies the provisions of the Convention". The first of the provisions to which I have referred expressly excludes the "general participation clause", i.e. the provision that the Convention will not apply unless all the belligerents are parties to it, which lessened the value of the Hague Conventions of 1899 and 1907. The second was intended to rule out a situation which occurred in the Second World War when Germany, although applying the Prisoners of War Convention to the treatment of the forces of another Power which was a party to the Convention – for instance, to British forces – declined, with terrible and disastrous effects, to apply it to the forces of a non-party, i.e. to the forces of the Soviet Union.

The third "common article" – Article 3 of each of the Conventions – is of the very greatest importance in the context of human rights. It applies to "an armed conflict not of an international character occurring in the territory of one of the Contracting Parties", and provides that each Party to such a conflict shall be bound to apply as a minimum certain provisions. These provisions are of such importance that I make no apology for quoting them in full. They are as follows:

(1) Persons taking no active part in the hostilities, including members of armed forces who have laid down their arms and those placed *hors de combat* by sickness, wounds, detention, or any other cause, shall in all circumstances be treated humanely, without any adverse distinction founded on race, colour, religion, or faith, sex, birth or wealth or any other similar criteria.

To this end, certain acts are prohibited in relation to such people "at any time and at any place whatsoever". These acts are:

   (a) violence to life and persons, in particular murder of all kinds, mutilation, cruel treatment and torture;
   (b) taking of hostages;
   (c) outrages upon personal dignity, in particular, humiliating and degrading treatment;
   (d) the passing of sentences and the carrying out of executions without previous judgement pronounced by a regularly constituted court affording all the judicial guarantees which are recognised as indispensable by civilised peoples.

Article 3 also provides that "the wounded and sick should be collected and cared for".

These provisions have been described as a Geneva "Convention" in miniature[8] and their purpose, essentially, is "to reduce the broad, essential humanitarian principles embodied in the rest of [each] Convention within the framework of one Article". The appearance in an international Convention of provisions binding not only states, but entities other than states, was a complete innovation. It should be noticed, in particular, that Article 3 was intentionally so drafted that its application in no way depends upon the recognition of the other Party to the conflict as a belligerent, either by outside states or by the legitimate government. This is emphasised by the last paragraph of Article 3, which states that "the application of the preceding provisions shall not affect the legal status of the parties to the conflict".

Writing shortly after the end of the 1949 Conference I expressed the opinion that Article 3 was "in accordance with the general trend of international law towards recognising that the question of the observance of fundamental human rights has ceased to be one of exclusive domestic jurisdiction of states",[9] and I should like at this point to endorse that opinion.

It would, of course, take a series of lectures, rather than just one lecture, to go right through the other provisions of the 1949 Convention in detail, and I do not, therefore, propose to do more than to indicate certain salient points in each Convention which particularly concern the protection of human rights.

[8] G. I. A. Draper, *The Red Cross Conventions*, p. 15.

[9] J. A. C. Gutteridge, "The Geneva Convention of 1949", *B.Y.B.I.L.*, 1949, p. 301.

In the 1949 "Wounded and Sick" Convention the salient articles are Articles 15, 16 and 17. Article 15 provides, *inter alia*, that "Parties to the conflict shall take all possible measures to search for and collect the wounded and sick, to protect them against pillage and ill-treatment" and "to ensure their adequate care". Article 15 also contains an obligation as to search for the dead and to prevent their being despoiled, an obligation which is reinforced by the obligations in Article 17 to ensure that the dead are honourably interred according to the rites of their religion. Article 18 recognises an obligation on the civilian population to "respect the wounded and sick and in particular to abstain from offering them violence".

Both the 1949 "Wounded and Sick" Convention and the corresponding Maritime Convention of that year contain (in Articles 46 and 47 respectively) an absolute prohibition of any reprisals against wounded, sick or shipwrecked persons, and personnel, buildings, equipment or vessels protected by the Convention.

The 1949 Prisoners of War Convention is, essentially, a recognition that "humane and decent treatment is a right and not a favour conferred on men and women of the armed forces who have been captured in the tide of war".[10] Since it is claimed at the present time that prisoner-of-war status should be enjoyed by guerillas and by "freedom fighters" in "national wars of liberation", it is important to recognise that the 1949 Prisoners of War Convention enumerates the categories of persons who are "prisoners of war in the sense of the Convention" if they have "fallen into the power of the enemy". These categories, which are all categories enumerated in the Hague Regulations with certain additions found to be necessary as the result of the experiences of the Second World War, are the following:

(1) Members of the armed forces of a Party to the conflict as well as members of militias or volunteer corps forming part of those forces;

(2) Members of other militias and volunteer corps, including those of organised resistance movements, if they fulfil the following conditions:

    (a) that of being commanded by a person responsible for his subordinates;

[10] Draper, *op. cit.*, p. 51.

    (b) that of having a fixed distinctive sign recognisable at a distance;

    (c) that of carrying arms openly;

    (d) that of conducting their operations in accordance with the laws and customs of war.

(3) Members of regular armed forces who profess allegiance to a government or authority not recognised by the Detaining Power.

(4) Persons who accompany the armed forces without actually being members thereof; e.g. war correspondents.

(5) Members of the merchant marine and crews of civil aircraft.

(6) Inhabitants of a non-occupied territory who, on the approach of the enemy spontaneously take up arms to resist the invading forces – provided they carry arms openly and respect the laws and customs of war – the *levée en masse*.

To ensure that humane and decent treatment is given to persons in the categories enumerated in Article 4 of the Prisoner of War Convention, Article 12 of the same Convention provides that prisoners of war are in the hands of the enemy power, and not of the individuals or units who have captured them, i.e., in other words, that the responsibility of the State is engaged if prisoners of war are ill-treated.

Article 13 provides that "prisoners of war must at all times be humanely treated" and expressly prohibits "any unlawful act or omission by the Detaining Power causing death or seriously endangering the health of a prisoner of war". Article 14 provides that prisoners of war are entitled in all circumstances to respect for their persons and their honour. Women are to be treated with all the regard due to their sex, and "should in all cases benefit by treatment as favourable as that granted to men". Measures of reprisal against prisoners of war are prohibited by Article 13.

Similar provisions to those I have just quoted are to be found in the Civilians Convention, but the great importance of that Convention is that for the first time detailed provisions have been included in an international Convention for safeguarding, in certain circumstances, the rights of civilians in time of war or any other armed conflict of an international character.

It is necessary to stress the words "in certain circumstances" because the title of the Convention is, perhaps, misleading. The Convention does not set out to protect *all* civilians in *all* circumstances in time of war or armed conflict, but, with the exception of Article 3, whose scope is in this particular respect wider, it protects only those civilians who are either in the territory of a belligerent or in occupied territory and who are neither nationals of the belligerent nor citizens of neutral states. Nor does the Convention attempt to protect civilians from the consequences of aerial bombardment, except, in Part II, to a very limited extent. There is, for example, in Article 18 of the Convention, a prohibition of attack on civilian hospitals organised to give care to the wounded and sick, the infirm and maternity cases, and a recommendation that such hospitals should be situated as far as possible from military objectives. There are also provisions (in Article 14) which *permit*, not oblige, states to establish hospital and safety zones and localities "so organised as to protect from the effect of war, wounded, sick and aged persons, children under fifteen, expectant mothers and mothers of children under seven". Such zones would be established in time of peace, but Article 15 would further permit neutralised zones to be established during a conflict by agreement between the belligerents, either direct or through a neutral state or "some humanitarian organisation". These neutralised zones would protect from the effects of war:

(a) wounded and sick combatants and non-combatants; and
(b) civilian persons who take no part in hostilities, and who while they reside in the zones, perform no work of a military character.

But outside hospital, safety and neutralised zones the presence of a protected person (as defined in the Convention) may not be used to render certain points or areas immune from military operation.

As well as the detailed provisions which apply, respectively, to the territories of the parties to the conflict and to occupied territories, the Civilian Convention contains, in Part III, provisions about the status and treatment of protected persons, which are common to both. Such persons are "entitled in all circumstances to respect for their persons, their honour, their family rights, their religious convictions and practices and their manners and customs". They are at all times to be humanely treated, and women are to be especially protected against any attack on their honour, in particular against rape, enforced prostitution, or any form of indecent assault. The following acts are also expressly prohibited by Articles 33 and 34 of the Convention:

collective penalties and all measures of intimidation or terrorism;
pillage;
reprisals.

There are also provisions in Part III of the Convention prohibiting individual or mass forcible transfers, as well as deportation
of protected persons from occupied territory to the territory of the
occupying Power or to that of any other country. These provisions
were inserted in the light of, and with vivid memories of, extensive
and inhumane deportations carried out by Germany in both world
wars.

It may, however, be asked at this point whether the Conventions
contain any effective sanctions against their breach. It is, therefore,
necessary to note that each Convention contains an Article under
which the Contracting Parties "undertake to enact any legislation
necessary to provide effective penal sanctions for and to bring to
trial persons committing, or ordering to be committed", certain
grave breaches of the Convention which are enumerated, in each
case, in a following Article. For example, these include in the case
of the Civilians Convention, "wilful killing, torture, or inhuman
treatment . . . unlawful deportations or transfer or unlawful con-
finement of a protected person . . . wilfully depriving a protected
person of the rights of fair and regular trial prescribed in the
Convention". In the United Kingdom the legislation enacted to
give effect to the "grave breaches" provisions of the Conventions
is to be found in the Geneva Conventions Act, 1957.

I have tried in the comparatively short time at my disposal to
summarise some of the main provisions of the 1949 Geneva
Conventions relating to the protection of human rights in time of
war. I should like to conclude by considering how far these
Conventions and other provisions of the Law of War to which I
have referred provide sufficiently adequate protection and in what
respects, if any, they are deficient.

At this point you should, I think, be aware of a resolution –
2444 (XXIII) – which the United Nations General Assembly
adopted in 1969. In paragraph 5 of that Resolution the General
Assembly called upon all states which had not yet done so to
become parties to the Hague Conventions of 1899 and 1907, the
Geneva Protocol of 1925, and the Geneva Convention of 1949. In
paragraph 1 the General Assembly affirmed a resolution adopted
by the 20th International Conference of the Red Cross in 1965

noting, *inter alia*, that "indiscriminate warfare is a danger for civilian populations and for the future of civilisation", and declaring that certain basic principles should be observed by every government and every authority conducting military operations. Three of these principles were specifically affirmed by the General Assembly. These are:

(a) that the right of the parties to a conflict to adopt means of injuring the enemy is not unlimited;

(b) that it is prohibited to launch attacks against the civilian population as such;

(c) that distinction must be made at all times between persons taking part in hostilities and members of the civilian population to the effect that the latter be spared as much as possible.

This resolution of the General Assembly appears to indicate that, despite the adoption of the 1949 Civilian Convention, the protection of the civilian population in general in time of war or any other armed conflict is still considered to be inadequate.

In so far as those who are specifically protected by the Civilians Convention are concerned – persons who in case of an international conflict or belligerent occupation "find themselves in the hands of a party to the conflict or occupying Power of which they are not nationals" – the protection afforded by the Convention is, as I have already indicated, a very considerable advance as compared with that afforded under international law as it existed before 1949. Up to a point, even a spy or saboteur *in occupied territory* is protected, since Article 5 of the Convention provides that "such persons shall . . . be treated with humanity and in the case of trial shall not be deprived of the rights of fair and regular trial provided by the Convention". This does not, of course, mean that a spy or guerrilla or any other "unprivileged combatant" who falls into the hands of an Occupying Power may not be executed if that is the penalty prescribed by the Occupying Power for the offence he is alleged to have committed, but it does mean that he cannot be executed summarily, and if his status is in doubt, e.g. if there is reasonable doubt as to whether or not he is a member of an organised resistance movement, Article 5 of the Prisoners of War Convention will apply and he will benefit from that Convention until his status has been determined.

But no protection is afforded under the Civilians Convention to nationals of the belligerents, and it is elsewhere that one must look in this case for the protection of human rights in time of war.

The International Covenant on Civil and Political Rights does not use the term "war" in permitting certain derogations from its provisions. It refers, however, to a time of public emergency threatening the life of the nation and it then allows certain derogations. Derogations are, however, not permitted from Article 6, which concerns the death penalty; and the circumstances under which it can be imposed; Article 7, which (like similar Articles in the Geneva Convention) prohibits "torture and cruel, inhumane or degrading treatment or punishment . . ."; Article 8, paragraphs 1 and 2, which prohibit slavery and practices akin to slavery; Article 11, which prohibits imprisonment solely on the ground of failure to fulfil a contractual obligation; Article 15, which provides that no person shall be held guilty of any criminal offence on account of any act or omission which did not constitute a criminal offence under national or international law at the time it was committed; Article 16 (recognition as a person); Article 18 (freedom of thought, conscience and religion). The Articles I have mentioned set out the human rights which *all* civilians would be entitled to enjoy in time of war in the territory of any belligerent. They apply, therefore, to nationals of the belligerent state and to neutrals in the territory of such a state, and the extent of protection is, therefore, in some respects, broader than that accorded under the 1949 Civilians Convention. The International Covenant on Civil and Political Rights has not yet entered into force, so it is also necessary to note that certain regional Human Rights Conventions – the European Convention and the similar American Convention – have provisions permitting derogations from the respective Conventions "in time of war or other public emergency . . . to the extent strictly required by the exigencies of the situation" and provided that such derogations are not inconsistent with the State's other obligations under international law (Article 15 (I) of the European Convention and Article 27 (I) of the American Convention).

Another respect in which the Civilians Convention is not, as we have seen, wholly adequate is in the protection, particularly against aerial bombardment, of civilians taking no part in the conflict. It is suggested in the two Reports prepared by the Secretary-General of the United Nations in accordance with General Assembly Resolution 2444 (XXIII) that greater consideration might be given for this purpose to the permissive provisions for the establishment of "hospital, safety and neutral zones" in Articles 14 and 15 of the 1949 Civilians Convention; it has also been suggested by Col. Draper in his work on *The Red Cross Conventions* that the provisions might even be of value in a conflict in which nuclear weapons were used.[11]

As far as the Prisoners of War Convention is concerned, the protection given to the men and women of the belligerents in an international conflict between states appears to be adequate. There are, however, certain difficulties of application arising from the nature of unified commands – i.e. command structures in which several states participate. Furthermore, as was shown in the Korea conflict, a new situation, not contemplated in the Geneva Convention, arises when military operations are conducted on one side by forces which are constituted under the aegis of the United Nations and are not, therefore, in a strict sense the forces of a Power which is a party to the Convention.

But apart from these difficulties, which are mainly difficulties of application, it has been claimed in several recent resolutions adopted by the United Nations General Assembly that in the case of what are called "colonial wars" the government administering the territory concerned should "ensure the application to the situation of the 1949 Prisoners of War Convention". In other words, guerrillas and other "freedom fighters" should be accorded the status of prisoners of war.

These resolutions, which are, of course, of a political nature, overlook, perhaps intentionally, that the 1949 Prisoners of War Convention is intended to apply, in its entirety, to conflicts between states, and thus to organised forces engaged in open warfare, and that it was Article 3 of that Convention alone which was intended to apply to conflicts of a non-international character. The sponsors of the United Nations Resolutions may also have overlooked the consideration that if guerrilla and freedom fighters in "colonial wars" are accorded the status of prisoners of war, the same status might be claimed for similar persons in armed conflicts the aim of which is secession from a parent state, e.g. for the Ibos in Nigeria during the Biafran conflict.

[11] Draper, *op. cit.*, p.p. 32–3.

It is, of course, the case that guerrillas and "freedom fighters" in non-international conflicts are already ensured a minimum of humane treatment under Article 3 of each of the 1949 Geneva Conventions. The difficulty here is that states have been reluctant since 1949 to admit that an Article 3 situation exists and have characterised outbreaks of violence as "internal disturbances", "terrorism", and so on, and not as armed conflict, in their territories. This has been so, even in cases in which there is little doubt that the minimum of humanitarian treatment for which Article 3 provides has, in fact, been given, e.g. in Cyprus and in Kenya before independence.

It is doubtful, however, whether the failure of states to admit that an Article 3 situation exists in their territories is, in itself, a sufficient justification for a claim that guerrillas and freedom fighters – persons who necessarily proceed by clandestine methods – should be given the full status of prisoners of war. They do not, in many cases, fulfil the requirements for organised resistance movements which, it will be recalled, are set out in Article 4 of the Prisoners of War Convention, e.g. the requirements of having a fixed distinctive sign recognisable at a distance and of carrying arms openly.

It has been suggested, and I would associate myself with this view, that to give such persons full prisoner-of-war status is neither consistent with the 1949 Convention as a whole, nor is it in the best interests of the civilian population involved in an internal conflict. It has been well said that the uniformed combatant confronted with a civilian in time of armed conflict – whether it be an international conflict or an internal conflict – will not know who is his adversary and who is not, and the whole of the civilian population may, therefore, be regarded as potential enemies and, therefore, as subject to attack and destruction. The slaughter of unarmed women, children and old men at My Lai is without any justification; it is, however, unhappily the case that such terrible incidents are more likely to take place if everyone in the civilian population is regarded as a potential enemy.

To say that guerrillas and freedom fighters should not be accorded the status of prisoners of war is not, however, to deny them all protection in the event of an internal conflict. It may be that Article 3 of the Geneva Conventions is too limited, not only in the protection it affords to "unprivileged" combatants, but also to the civilian population as a whole.

There may be circumstances in which further protection than that at present afforded by Article 3 of the Geneva Conventions should be given to members of organised resistance movements in conflicts which are not of an international character, e.g. if they fulfil some, but not necessarily all, of the requirements listed in Article 4 of the Prisoners of War Convention. There might, for instance, have been a case for according such further protection to the Ibos in the Biafran conflict, whose forces conducted open operations. There would also appear to be a strong case, and this is stressed by the My Lai massacres, for ensuring a greater measure of protection to civilians in conflicts which are claimed to be of an internal nature but in which one or both sides is receiving military assistance from other states.

The remedy is not, however, I submit, an extension of the existing Geneva Conventions to circumstances to which they were not – with the exception of Article 3 – intended to apply – a solution which appears to be envisaged not only in the "political" resolutions of the United Nations General Assembly, but also in a Resolution of the Teheran Conference on Human Rights and in Resolution XVIII of the XXIst International Conference of the Red Cross. It is, rather, the formulation of a new Convention or Conventions for the protection of victims in the case of an armed conflict of a non-international character and the application in good faith of the rules thus formulated by all parties to the conflict. In this way the basic concept implicit in the first of the Red Cross Conventions might be translated into provisions expressly designed to meet new situations and new circumstances.

Extract from the Bill of Rights, 1688

"And thereupon the said Lords Spiritual and Temporal, and Commons, pursuant to their respective Letters and Elections, being now assembled in a full and free Representative of this Nation, taking into their most serious Consideration the best Means for attaining the Ends aforesaid; do in the first Place (as their Ancestors in like Case have usually done) for the vindicating and asserting their ancient Rights and Liberties, declare;

1. That the pretended Power of suspending of Laws, or the Execution of Laws, by regal Authority, without Consent of Parliament, is illegal.

2. That the pretended Power of dispensing with Laws, or the Execution of Laws, by regal Authority, as it hath been assumed and exercised of late, is illegal.

3. That the Commission for erecting the late Court of Commissioners for Ecclesiastical Causes, and all other Commissions and Courts of like Nature, are illegal and pernicious.

4. That levying Money for or to the Use of the Crown, by Pretence of Prerogative, without Grant of Parliament, for longer Time, or in other Manner than the same is or shall be granted, is illegal.

5. That it is the Right of the Subjects to petition the King, and all Commitments and Prosecutions for such petitioning are illegal.

6. That the raising or keeping a Standing Army within the Kingdom in Time of Peace, unless it be with Consent of Parliament, is against Law.

7. That the Subjects which are Protestants, may have Arms for their Defence suitable to their Conditions, and as allowed by Law.

8. That Election of Members of Parliament ought to be free.

9. That the Freedom of Speech, and Debates or Proceedings in Parliament, ought not to be impeached or questioned in any Court or Place out of Parliament.

10. That excessive Bail ought not to be required, nor excessive Fines imposed; nor cruel and unusual Punishments inflicted.

11. That Jurors ought to be duly impanelled and returned, and Jurors which pass upon Men in Trials for High Treason ought to be Freeholders.

12. That all Grants and Promises of Fines and Forfeitures of particular Persons before Conviction, are illegal and void.

13. And that for Redress of all Grievances, and for the amending, strengthening, and preserving of the Laws, Parliaments ought to be held frequently.

And they do claim, demand, and insist upon all and singular the Premises, as their undoubted Rights and Liberties; and that no Declarations, Judgements, Doings, or Proceedings, to the Prejudice of the People in any of the said Premises, ought in any wise to be drawn hereafter into Consequence or Example."

Universal Declaration of Human Rights Approved by the General Assembly of the United Nations

Paris, 10 *December* 1948

PREAMBLE

WHEREAS recognition of the inherent dignity and of the equal and inalienable rights of all members of the human family is the foundation of freedom, justice and peace in the world,

WHEREAS disregard and contempt for human rights have resulted in barbarous acts which have outraged the conscience of mankind, and the advent of a world in which human beings shall enjoy freedom of speech and belief and freedom from fear and want has been proclaimed as the highest aspiration of the common people,

WHEREAS it is essential, if man is not to be compelled to have recourse, as a last resort, to rebellion against tyranny and oppression, that human rights should be protected by the rule of law,

WHEREAS it is essential to promote the development of friendly relations between nations,

WHEREAS, the peoples of the United Nations have in the Charter[1] reaffirmed their faith in fundamental human rights, in the dignity and worth of the human person and in the equal rights of men and women and have determined to promote social progress and better standards of life in larger freedom.

WHEREAS Member States have pledged themselves to achieve, in co-operation with the United Nations, the promotion of universal respect for and observance of human rights and fundamental freedoms,

WHEREAS a common understanding of these rights and freedoms is of the greatest importance for the full realisation of this pledge.

NOW, THEREFORE,

THE GENERAL ASSEMBLY,

PROCLAIMS this Universal Declaration of Human Rights as a common standard of achievement for all peoples and all nations, to the end that every individual and every organ of society, keeping

[1] "Treaty Series No. 67 (1946)", Cmd. 7015.

this Declaration constantly in mind, shall strive by teaching and education to promote respect for these rights and freedoms and by progressive measures, national and international, to secure their universal and effective recognition and observance, both among the peoples of Member States themselves and among the peoples of territories under their jurisdiction.

ARTICLE 1

All human beings are born free and equal in dignity and rights. They are endowed with reason and conscience and should act towards one another in a spirit of brotherhood.

ARTICLE 2

Everyone is entitled to all the rights and freedoms set forth in this Declaration, without distinction of any kind, such as race, colour, sex, language, religion, political or other opinion, national or social origin, property, birth or other status.

Furthermore, no distinction shall be made on the basis of the political, jurisdictional or international status of the country or territory to which a person belongs, whether it be independent, trust, non-self-governing or under any other limitation of sovereignty.

ARTICLE 3

Everyone has the right to life, liberty and the security of person.

ARTICLE 4

No one shall be held in slavery or servitude; slavery and the slave trade shall be prohibited in all their forms.

ARTICLE 5

No one shall be subjected to torture or to cruel, inhuman or degrading treatment or punishment.

ARTICLE 6

Everyone has the right to recognition everywhere as a person before the law.

ARTICLE 7

All are equal before the law and are entitled without any discrimination to equal protection of the law. All are entitled to equal protection against any discrimination in violation of this Declaration and against any incitement to such discrimination.

ARTICLE 8

Everyone has the right to an effective remedy by the competent national tribunals for acts violating the fundamental rights granted him by the constitution or by law.

ARTICLE 9

No one shall be subjected to arbitrary arrest, detention or exile.

ARTICLE 10

Everyone is entitled in full equality to a fair and public hearing by an independent and impartial tribunal, in the determination of his rights and obligations and of any criminal charge against him.

ARTICLE 11

1. Everyone charged with a penal offence has the right to be presumed innocent until proved guilty according to law in a public trial at which he has had all the guarantees necessary for his defence.

2. No one shall be held guilty of any penal offence on account of any act or omission which did not constitute a penal offence, under national or international law, at the time when it was committed. Nor shall a heavier penalty be imposed than the one that was applicable at the time the penal offence was committed.

ARTICLE 12

No one shall be subjected to arbitrary interference with his privacy, family, home or correspondence, nor to attacks upon his honour and reputation. Everyone has the right to the protection of the law against such interference or attacks.

ARTICLE 13

1. Everyone has the right to freedom of movement and residence within the borders of each State.

2. Everyone has the right to leave any country, including his own, and to return to his country.

ARTICLE 14

1. Everyone has the right to seek and to enjoy in other countries asylum from persecution.

2. This right may not be invoked in the case of prosecutions genuinely arising from non-political crimes or from acts contrary to the purpose and principles of the United Nations.

ARTICLE 15

1. Everyone has the right to a nationality.

2. No one shall be arbitrarily deprived of his nationality nor denied the right to change his nationality.

ARTICLE 16

1. Men and women of full age, without any limitation due to race, nationality or religion, have the right to marry and to found a family. They are entitled to equal rights as to marriage, during marriage and at its dissolution.

2. Marriage shall be entered into only with the free and full consent of the intending spouses.

3. The family is the natural and fundamental group unit of society and is entitled to protection by society and the State.

ARTICLE 17

1. Everyone has the right to own property alone as well as in association with others.

2. No one shall be arbitrarily deprived of his property.

ARTICLE 18

Everyone has the right to freedom of thought, conscience and religion; this right includes freedom to change his religion or belief, and freedom, either alone or in community with others and in public or private, to manifest his religion or belief in teaching, practice, worship and observance.

ARTICLE 19

Everyone has the right to freedom of opinion and expression; this right includes freedom to hold opinions without interference and to seek, receive and impart information and ideas through any media and regardless of frontiers.

ARTICLE 20

1. Everyone has the right to freedom of peaceful assembly and association.

2. No one may be compelled to belong to an association.

ARTICLE 21

1. Everyone has the right to take part in the government of his country, directly or through freely chosen representatives.

2. Everyone has the right of equal access to public service in his country.

3. The will of the people shall be the basis of the authority of government; this will shall be expressed in periodic and genuine elections which shall be by universal and equal suffrage and shall be held by secret vote or equivalent free voting procedures.

ARTICLE 22

Everyone, as a member of society, has the right to social security and is entitled to the realisation, through national effort and international co-operation and in accordance with the organisation and resources of each State, of the economic, social and cultural rights indispensable for his dignity and the free development of his personality.

ARTICLE 23

1. Everyone has the right to work, to free choice of employment, to just and favourable conditions of work and to protection against unemployment.

2. Everyone, without any discrimination, has the right to equal pay for equal work.

3. Everyone who works has the right to just and favourable remuneration insuring for himself and his family an existence worthy of human dignity, and supplemented, if necessary, by other means of social protection.

4. Everyone has the right to form and to join trade unions for the protection of his interests.

ARTICLE 24

Everyone has the right to rest and leisure, including reasonable limitation of working hours and periodic holidays with pay.

ARTICLE 25

1. Everyone has the right to a standard of living adequate for the health and well-being of himself and of his family, including food, clothing, housing and medical care and necessary social services, and the right to security in the event of unemployment,

sickness, disability, widowhood, old age or other lack of liveli-
hood in circumstances beyond his control.

2. Motherhood and childhood are entitled to special care and
assistance. All children, whether born in or out of wedlock, shall
enjoy the same social protection.

ARTICLE 26

1. Everyone has the right to education. Education shall be free,
at least in the elementary and fundamental stages. Elementary
education shall be compulsory. Technical and professional education shall be made generally available and higher education shall
be equally accessible to all on the basis of merit.

2. Education shall be directed to the full development of the
human personality and to the strengthening of respect for human
rights and fundamental freedoms. It shall promote understanding,
tolerance and friendship among all nations, racial or religious
groups, and shall further the activities of the United Nations for
the maintenance of peace.

3. Parents have a prior right to choose the kind of education
that shall be given to their children.

ARTICLE 27

1. Everyone has the right freely to participate in the cultural
life of the community, to enjoy the arts and to share in scientific
advancement and its benefits.

2. Everyone has the right to the protection of the moral and
material interests resulting from any scientific, literary or artistic
production of which he is the author.

ARTICLE 28

Everyone is entitled to a social and international order in which
the rights and freedoms set forth in this Declaration can be fully
realised.

ARTICLE 29

1. Everyone has duties to the community in which alone the
free and full development of his personality is possible.

2. In the exercise of his rights and freedoms, everyone shall be
subject only to such limitations as are determined by law solely
for the purpose of securing due recognition and respect for the

rights and freedoms of others and of meeting the just requirements of morality, public order and the general welfare in a democratic society.

3. These rights and freedoms may in no case be exercised contrary to the purposes and principles of the United Nations.

ARTICLE 30

Nothing in this Declaration may be interpreted as implying for any State, group or person any right to engage in any activity or to perform any act aimed at the destruction of any of the rights and freedoms set forth herein.

Bibliography

Political Theory
PLATO: *The Republic.*
ARISTOTLE: *Politics.*
MACHIAVELLI: *The Prince.*
GROTIUS: *De jure belli ac pacis.*
HOBBES: *Leviathan.*
LOCKE: *Two Treatises on Government.*
ROUSSEAU: *Discourse on Inequality.*
  Social Contract.
BENTHAM: *Fragment on Government.*
  Introduction to the Principles of Morals and Legislation.
SABINE, G. H.: *A History of Political Theory* (Harrap).

Constitutional Law
DICEY, A. V.: *Law of the Constitution* (Macmillan).
FRANCK, T. M.: *Comparative Constitutional Process; Cases and Materials* (Sweet & Maxwell).
HART, W. O.: *Introduction to the Law of Local Government and Administration* (Butterworth).
DE SMITH, S. A.: *Constitutional and Administrative Law* (Penguin).
STREET, H.: *Freedom, the Individual and the Law* (Penguin).
WADE & PHILLIPS: *Constitutional Law* (Longman).
WILLIAMS, D.: *Keeping the Peace* (Hutchinson).

Commonwealth
EZEJIOFOR, G. O.: *Protection of Human Rights under the Law* (Butterworth).
DE SMITH, S. A.: *The New Commonwealth and its Constitution* (Stevens).
USA
CHANNING, E.: *The United States of America* 1765–1865 (Cambridge).

EMERSON, HABER AND DORSEN: *Political and Civil Rights in the United States* (Little, Brown & Co., Boston).

SCHWARTZ, B.: *A Commentary on the Constitution of the United States*, 1963–68 (Macmillan, New York).

SCHWARTZ, B.: *American Constitutional Law* (Cambridge University Press, England).

Human Rights

Historical and Political Background

LESTER, A.: *Democracy and Individual Rights* (Fabian Tract 390).

MOSKOWITZ, M.: *Human Rights and World Order* (Oceana).

MOSKOWITZ, M.: *The Politics and Dynamics of Human Rights* (Oceana).

REMEC, P. P.: *The Position of the Individual in International Law according to Grotius and Vattel* (Nijhoff).

VERZIJL, J. H. W.: *Human Rights in Historical Perspective* (Joh. Enschadé en Zonen, Haarlem).

General

BROWNLIE, I.: *Basic Documents on Human Rights* (Oxford).[1]

JENKS, C. W.: *The Common Law of Mankind* (Stevens).

JENKS, C. W.: *Human Rights and International Labour Standards* (London Institute of World Affairs).

LAUTERPACHT, H.; *International Law and Human Rights* (Stevens).

LUARD, E. (Ed.): *The International Protection of Human Rights* (Thames and Hudson).

INTERNATIONAL INSTITUTE OF HUMAN RIGHTS (RENÉ CASSIN FOUNDATION): *René Cassin, Amicorum Discipulorumque Liber, – Problèmes de Protection Internationale des Droits de l'Homme*[2] (A. Pedone, Paris).

ROBERTSON, A. H. (Ed.): *Human Rights in National and International Law* (Manchester).

ROBERTSON, A. H.: *Human Rights in the World* (Manchester).

also

HUMAN RIGHTS – JOURNAL OF INTERNATIONAL AND COMPARATIVE LAW- Editor-in-Chief, K. Vasak.

[1] See also the numerous references in the headnotes to the documents.
[2] A collection of essays in English and French.

OFFICIAL RECORDS OF THE UNITED NATIONS: RECORDS OF THE HUMAN RIGHTS COMMISSION, THE ECONOMIC AND SOCIAL COUNCIL AND THE GENERAL ASSEMBLY.

UNITED NATIONS YEARBOOK OF HUMAN RIGHTS.

European

ANTONOPOULOS, N.: *La jurisprudence des organes de la convention européenne des droits de l'homme* (Sijthoff).

FAWCETT, J. E. S.: *The Application of the European Convention on Human Rights*[3] (Oxford).

MONCONDUIT, F.: *La commission européenne des droits de l'homme* (Sijthoff).

MORRISSON, C. C., JR.: *The Developing European Law of Human Rights* (Sijthoff).

ROBERTSON, A. H.: *Human Rights in Europe* (Manchester).

VASAK, K.: *La convention européenne des droits de l'homme* (Pichon et Durand-Auzias, Paris).

WEIL, G.: *The European Convention on Human Rights* (Sijthoff).

also

DECISIONS OF THE EUROPEAN COMMISSION OF HUMAN RIGHTS, 1955–.

DIGEST OF CASE-LAW RELATING TO THE EUROPEAN CONVENTION ON HUMAN RIGHTS, 1955–1967 (Printed in Belgium but correspondence relating to the Digest should be addressed to the Directorate of Human Rights, Council of Europe, Strasbourg, France).

JUDGMENTS, PLEADINGS, AND DOCUMENTS OF THE EUROPEAN COURT OF HUMAN RIGHTS.

EUROPEAN CONVENTION ON HUMAN RIGHTS – COLLECTED TEXTS (Published in Strasbourg).

YEARBOOK OF THE EUROPEAN CONVENTION ON HUMAN RIGHTS (Nijhoff).

---

[3] Appendix 3 contains a useful chronological list of selected sources and materials from 1950 to 1968 including a number of important articles in various periodicals.